FRAMEWORKS

MODERN

WONDERS

Shana Priwer

Cynthia Phillips

Routledge
Taylor & Francis Group
LONDON AND NEW YORK

First published 2009 by M.E. Sharpe

Published 2015 by Routledge
4 Park Square, Milton Park, Abingdon, Oxon OX14 4RN
605 Third Avenue, New York, NY 10017

Routledge is an imprint of the Taylor & Francis Group, an informa business

Copyright © 2009 Taylor & Francis. All rights reserved.

No part of this book may be reprinted or reproduced or utilised in any form or by any electronic, mechanical, or other means, nowknown or hereafter invented, including photocopying and recording, or in anyinformation storage or retrieval system, without permission in writing from the publishers.

Notices
No responsibility is assumed by the publisher for any injury and/or damage to persons or property as a matter of products liability, negligence or otherwise, or from any use of operation of any methods, products, instructions or ideas contained in the material herein.

Practitioners and researchers must always rely on their own experience and knowledge in evaluating and using any information, methods, compounds, or experiments described herein. In using such information or methods they should be mindful of their own safety and the safety of others, including parties for whom they have a professional responsibility.

Product or corporate names may be trademarks or registered trademarks, and are used only for identification and explanation without intent to infringe.

Library of Congress Cataloging-in-Publication Data

Modern wonders / Cynthia Phillips and Shana Priwer.
    p. cm. -- (Frameworks)
 Includes bibliographical references and index.
 ISBN 978-0-7656-8124-9 (hardcover : alk. paper)
 1. Architecture, Modern--Juvenile literature. 2. Architecture and technology--Juvenile literature. I. Priwer, Shana. II. Title.

NA680.P3786 2008
724'.6--dc22

                          2007040700

Editor: Peter Mavrikis
Production Manager: Henrietta Toth
Editorial Assistant and Photo Research: Alison Morretta
Program Coordinator: Cathy Prisco
Design: Patrice Sheridan
Line Art: FoxBytes

PHOTO CREDITS: Cover: Dorling Kindersley/Getty Images; title page: Taxi/Getty Images; pages 6, 17, 65, 78, 84, 86, 89 (middle right): Hulton Archive/Getty Images; pages 8, 13, 33, 101: Photographer's Choice/Getty Images; pages 9, 36, 43, 54, 56, 87: Stone/Getty Images; pages 10, 11 (top), 31, 38, 45, 52, 64, 66, 67 (top), 67 (bottom), 68, 77, 96, 100: FoxBytes; page 11 (bottom): Lonely Planet Images/Getty Images; pages 15, 57: AFP/Getty Images; page 16: Adoc-photos/Art Resource, NY; page 19: Sebun Photo/Getty Images; pages 20, 26, 39: Taxi/Getty Images; page 21: National Geographic/Getty Images; pages 22, 90: Gallo Images/Getty Images; pages 24, 76: Time & Life Pictures/Getty Images; page 27: Associated Press; pages 29, 41, 46, 50, 55, 62, 72: Getty Images; page 34: Robert Harding World Imagery/Getty Images; page 40: Tim Graham Photo Library/Getty Images; page 58: First Light/Getty Images; page 61: Scala/Art Resource, NY; pages 81, 83, 92: Library of Congress; pages 89 (far left), 89 (middle left): The Bridgeman Art Library/Getty Images; page 89 (far right): Popperfoto/Getty Images; page 99: De Agostini Picture Library/Getty Images; back cover: Photographer's Choice/Getty Images.

ISBN 13: 978-0-7656-8200-0 (pbk)

CONTENTS

	About Frameworks	4
Chapter 1	ACHIEVEMENT IN IRON: THE EIFFEL TOWER	7
Chapter 2	CELEBRATION OF EXPANSION: THE ST. LOUIS GATEWAY ARCH	23
Chapter 3	CURVILINEAR DESIGN	37
Chapter 4	WORKING COLD: ARCHITECTURE ON ICE	51
Chapter 5	REBUILDING A SYMBOL: THE WORLD TRADE CENTER	63
Chapter 6	STONE GIANTS: MOUNT RUSHMORE NATIONAL MEMORIAL	79
Chapter 7	ROUND THEY GO: THE MILLENNIUM WHEEL	91
	Glossary	103
	Find Out More	107
	Index	109

ABOUT FRAMEWORKS

Architecture has undergone sweeping development since the beginning of time. In biblical days, most architecture was temporary because it accommodated a nomadic population. As communities began to grow roots, so did their architecture. Whether it was residential, commercial, religious, or civic, structures of permanence slowly appeared on the global landscape.

Over time, specific aesthetics and structural techniques were developed. The knowledge of physical sciences became more advanced and, as a result, engineers responded by creating increasingly complex works that challenged previous notions. Temples became more elaborate, buildings grew ever taller, and bridges spanned bodies of water that only boats had dared to cross before. Once science and design crossed paths, there was no turning back.

The goal of the FRAMEWORKS series is to provide insight into the science behind the structures that are part of our everyday lives. Dams require advanced hydroelectric technology; the Egyptian pyramids paved new paths in the transport of stone and the construction of stone structures. Basic concepts from mathematics, physics, and engineering help illustrate the science that supports the creation of increasingly complex structures.

This series assumes no prior knowledge of advanced math and physics, but rather builds up the reader's understanding by explaining scientific concepts in words as well as equations. Engaging examples are used to illustrate ideas such as mass, force, speed, and energy. Case studies from real-world projects demonstrate the concepts. Famous disasters also serve an important purpose

ABOUT FRAMEWORKS

in showing how even for professional architects and engineers, gaining knowledge is a slow and gradual task.

MODERN WONDERS describes several of the crowning architectural achievements of recent centuries. Steel was a major factor in the creation of the Eiffel Tower. Without steel and other essential engineering advances, this tower and subsequent skyscrapers would never have been possible. Another amazing structure, the St. Louis Gateway Arch, took building with steel to new levels.

Curvilinear buildings, where curved rather than straight lines define part or all of the structure, have become increasingly popular in recent years, in large part due to advances in computer software that allow for their design and fabrication. The Sydney Opera House is an example of a project that took advantage of engineering and construction technology and managed to respect the intended use of the space at the same time. The Bilbao Guggenheim Museum, on the other hand, was made possible by computer-aided design and manufacturing software that was not available at the time that the Sydney Opera House was built. It was not possible to produce building elements that curved simultaneously in multiple directions on a large scale prior to recent developments in computer design technology.

Unfortunately, some masterful architectural achievements have fallen to terrorism or other disasters. The Twin Towers of the World Trade Center in New York City pushed the field of skyscraper design to new heights, both literally and figuratively. They were the subjects of two other disasters before their ultimate demise in the terrorist attacks of September 11, 2001, and the site where they stood is currently the focus of a major rebuilding effort.

Some engineering wonders are not intended for habitation. Mount Rushmore is a massive sculpture carved into the South Dakota Black Hills. It commemorates the achievements of the nation in a way that also celebrates the natural landscape. Similarly, large amusement park rides such as the Millennium Eye in London simultaneously celebrate engineering achievement, materials innovation, and creative ingenuity. The range of impressive designs in recent centuries is a testament to the expertise of the people involved in every aspect of these building projects—from the development of materials down to the last detail of construction.

The FRAMEWORKS series provides an entertaining and educational approach to the science of building. Read on to learn about the ways in which science supports, literally, our built environment.

CHAPTER 1

ACHIEVEMENT IN IRON

The Eiffel Tower

The driving force behind new architectural works can come from a number of sources. Famous and wealthy individuals sometimes sponsor monuments to commemorate their lives, cities sponsor new development in the interest of encouraging the local economy, and architectural masterpieces can even be created purely for showmanship and competition.

The Eiffel Tower fits into the last category. This building was designed and created exclusively for the Paris Exposition of 1889, and had it not been for the building's proven usefulness, it likely would have been torn down after the main event. The exposition was held on the centennial of the French Revolution and included exhibits and temporary structures to celebrate French achievements.

A design competition was held to solicit proposals for a signature structure and more than 700 entries were received. These entries included a design for a 985-foot (300-meter) tall guillotine. In a unanimous vote of approval, the design of engineer Alexandre-Gustave Eiffel was selected for production. Eiffel's partners in the competition and construction phase were architect Stephen Sauvestre and the engineering team of Emile Nouguier and Maurice Koechlin.

The Eiffel Tower is considered a national treasure today, but in the nineteenth century many saw it as an eyesore. During construction, when it

Engineer Gustave Eiffel stands below the Eiffel Tower during its construction in 1888.

MODERN WONDERS

became clear how large the tower was intended to be, several prominent citizens spoke out and declared the structure to be aesthetically hideous. It was also thought that the building was tall enough that it might interfere with the migratory patterns of Parisian birds! Fortunately construction proceeded despite these objections.

One of the most obvious differences between the Eiffel Tower and a modern skyscraper is the lack of cladding. Buildings intended primarily for human occupation have walls, insulation, windows, and other elements designed to protect and comfort the inhabitants. The Eiffel Tower, while usable as a viewing station, was never designed as full-time shelter. Thus, it presents a clean image of its structural integrity without hiding these elements behind a facade.

The Eiffel Tower, today an icon of the Parisian skyline, was actually considered an eyesore when it was first built.

Materials

When it was built, the Eiffel Tower was the world's largest building. It held that title until the Chrysler Building was constructed in New York in 1930. It was also the largest building of the day to be created from puddled iron. This high-quality iron is created from pig iron, or crude iron. Puddling is a technique that involves the melting, casting, and reheating of iron to remove as many impurities as possible. The iron is then rolled, stacked, and cut multiple times to increase its density and strength.

The tower's structure consists of an interlocking network of iron lattice frames. Iron bars were placed into trusses, which were then integrated with other members to form one massive lattice.

As one of the initial steps in casting beams, liquid iron is poured into a mold.

MODERN WONDERS

The Eiffel Tower had to be designed to withstand not only the vertical load of the heavy iron structure, but also the varying horizontal forces from wind.

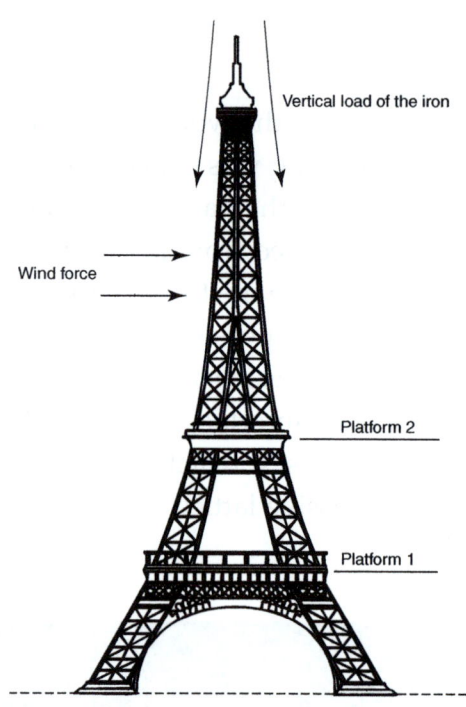

At first glance, the Eiffel Tower appears to be drastically overengineered. Were all of the lattice pieces really necessary for the structure to stand? Part of the answer lies in the nature of cast iron, which does not have the same strength in tension that modern steel does. One of the most important features of steel is that it has nearly equal strength in both tension (a pulling force that acts to stretch the object under force) and compression (a pushing force that applies pressure to the object under force).

Since puddled iron was still a fairly weak material despite the nature of its manufacturing, Eiffel added more reinforcements than were probably necessary. In addition, the intricate nature of the lattice contributed to the overall aesthetic of the structure, one that embodied technology, grace, and industry. The structure and design of the tower were highly intermingled.

The overall shape of the Eiffel Tower resulted from a careful study of physics, drawing on Eiffel's background in aerodynamics. Each of the four piers at the base of the structure would be under a significant vertical load from the weight of the iron above it. In addition, wind creates a horizontal force that is also transferred down to the piers, which are considerably larger and more resistant than the more delicate upper portion of the tower. The curved shape of the legs at the base is such that both the horizontal and vertical forces are properly deflected.

STRUCTURE

The foundations for the tower were excavated to a depth of about 52 feet (16 meters) and were filled with limestone and concrete. Massive anchor

ACHIEVEMENT IN IRON

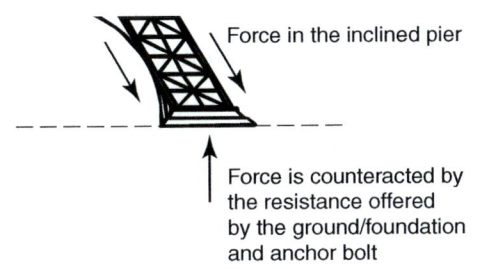

Inclined piers at the base of the Eiffel Tower were anchored deeply into the ground and designed to counterbalance the horizontal and vertical forces in the tower.

bolts measuring 25 feet (7.5 meters) long were set into each foundation. The bottom construction pieces were then built from these bolts. The bolts, plus the resistance from the ground and foundation, helped to offset the axial force (force acting along an axis) that was present in the slanted piers.

The overall height of the Eiffel Tower is 1,052 feet (320 meters). The structure is divided into essentially two parts: base and tower. The base portion was constructed using four massive pillars. These were built separately and then placed about 260 feet (80 meters) apart from each other.

The open trusswork of the Eiffel Tower was intended as both a structurally sound and aesthetically beautiful design element.

Trusses were utilized extensively in the fabrication of the base. Because these portions all slanted inward, construction was difficult until the piers were connected together to form a unified base. The tower portions required less challenging construction, as they were built directly from the base.

The project required a massive manpower effort. More than 300 steelworkers were involved and their efforts occupied a full two years of labor. The project required more than 18,000 iron bars connected with more than 2.5 million rivets—not a small project by any stretch of the imagination!

Workers were able to keep the project moving efficiently by using steam-driven cranes.

11

These were based on the principle of the steam-powered engine, in which steam that is pumped into a cylinder and cooled creates a vacuum. When steam condenses into water, the material changes in density (since water is much denser than steam) and therefore in volume. The atmospheric pressure in the engine chamber is greatly reduced, causing a piston at the top of the chamber to travel downward. It is the motion of this piston, which moves up as more steam is added and then down as it condenses, that drives the engine. Similar systems were used to drive steam engines on trains and other machinery in the early Industrial Revolution.

The French steam-driven cranes were effective until the structure was too tall for the cranes to reach. From that point on, creeper cranes were used to aid in the rest of the construction. These were specially designed cranes that crawled up the vertical elevator tracks in order to transport iron pieces up to the level of the workers. Because the iron used in the tower was created off-site to the precise dimensions required, the workers up in the tower simply assembled the pieces that were delivered, much like a three-dimensional jigsaw puzzle.

ASSEMBLY

Skilled ironworkers installed the iron bars. The life of the ironworker was far from easy for two major reasons: temperature and height. The Eiffel Tower was a year-round project for most of its two-year construction, and the ironworkers had to be outside, rain or shine, in broiling heat or freezing cold. They also had to work hundreds of feet above the ground.

While more than half of the iron used to create the Eiffel Tower was assembled and riveted on the ground, many pieces had to be riveted in position. Rivets are metal pins with a large head at one end that are designed to connect two or more objects together. The rivet is pushed through holes in the pieces of metal that are to be connected. The head at the opposite end of the rivet is hammered flat to firmly connect the pieces together.

Typically, when connecting rivets in on-site construction, ironworkers first bolt or otherwise grip the metal pieces together. A rivet is inserted and the end is heated enough to make it malleable. The end is then

ACHIEVEMENT IN IRON

pounded to form a second head that is shaped properly with a riveting tool and then allowed to cool. The ironworker removes the temporary bolts and moves on to the next rivet.

ELEVATORS

Elevators were a key requirement to allow human access to the Eiffel Tower. The Otis Elevator Company performed the elevator work for the tower. It was a challenging project because the portions of the elevator that ran through the pier legs had to travel at an incline rather than a straight vertical rise, as is typical for elevators. The design used a steam-powered cylinder to raise and lower the elevator car. This system was upgraded and replaced with an electric one about 1910. In the 1980s the existing elevators were replaced with double-decker elevator cars, increasing the overall efficiency of the elevator system.

Stairs are available for those who do not want to use the elevator—1,665 of

The elevators at the core of the Eiffel Tower were designed to move up and down along the axis of the inclined legs. This unique movement enabled passengers to travel to viewing platforms located at different levels throughout the tower.

13

> ## CONSTRUCTION SAFETY
>
> Construction of the Eiffel Tower was a risky endeavor. In typical skyscraper construction, a worker who falls in toward the center of the building would likely be stopped by the floor beneath. In the case of the Eiffel Tower there were only two platforms for the entire seventy-five–story height. Due to the designers' creative use of scaffolding and rails, however, only one worker lost his life over the course of the entire project.

them. However, the stairs that are open to the public do not go all the way up to the top of the tower, but stop at the second level.

Beyond the 1889 Exposition

Once its duties as an exposition masterpiece were completed, the Eiffel Tower began its long-standing job as a radio tower. The south pillar eventually housed a radio center, and in the 1950s television and FM radio were transmitted via the tower.

Radio waves allow the functionality of everything from radio and television to baby monitors, cell phones, GPS receivers, and even garage-door openers. Radio waves are part of the electromagnetic spectrum, which ranges from short-wavelength, high-energy radiation such as ultraviolet and X-rays, to visible light in the mid-range, down to longer-wavelength radiation as found in microwaves and radio waves. Long-wavelength radiation is ideal for signals to travel over large distances with relatively low power, but the tradeoff is that very large antennas can be necessary to transmit and receive radio signals. Tall radio towers allow signals to travel in all directions without being

ACHIEVEMENT IN IRON

blocked by other objects. Radio transmitters are often placed on hilltops or tall buildings.

As the tallest structure available, the Eiffel Tower was an ideal spot for a radio transmitter. Antennae were run from the tower down to the base and were functional until a permanent radio control center was built on the site in the early 1950s. Another permanent radio antenna was added in 1959.

MAINTAINING THE STRUCTURE

The Eiffel Tower has had several facelifts over the years. As early as 1900 an additional level was added. By 1902 the spire required structural reinforcement, which was needed again in the 1970s. In 1981 a major renovation of the Eiffel Tower involved structural reinforcement for television and radio equipment, the creation of supporting structures for new elevators, and the construction of a restaurant. A lighting system was unveiled in 1986, which made the tower stand out against the night sky.

The Eiffel Tower is illuminated with 20,000 bulbs, enough to create a particularly spectacular display at nighttime.

Biography of Alexandre-Gustave Eiffel

The engineer responsible for the iconic Eiffel Tower, Alexandre-Gustave Eiffel, was born in 1832 in Dijon, France. He was trained in Paris, attending the Ecole Polytechnique and Ecole Central, and soon began a prolific design career. His first job was with a bridge company, and this was work that he continued to pursue in years to come.

The Eiffel Tower may have been Eiffel's crowning achievement, but it was certainly not the only engineering feat to which he contributed. He designed many bridges, as well as viaducts and other structures, in his lifetime. One well-known Eiffel bridge is the Ponte Maria Pia, a railway bridge he designed in Portugal to span the Douro River in 1877.

The Ponte Maria Bridge, in Portugal, shows some of the same wrought iron girder designs that would later be used in Eiffel's tower.

The bridge formed a crescent shape and was constructed of wrought iron, and the work clearly had an influence on his later namesake tower. He was also the engineer for Chile's Estacion Central, a railway station, as well as numerous iron bridges and structures in Peru, Hungary, Brazil, and other countries.

Eiffel's influence crossed the Atlantic Ocean. For New York City's Statue of Liberty, he designed the armature—the internal structural system around which the statue was created. Eiffel came up with a wrought iron framework that supported the copper skin. He was less successful in his subsequent negotiations with the French Panama Canal Company. In 1887 discussions were under way to construct a canal in Panama, and Eiffel had a keen interest in its design. However, Eiffel ran into legal troubles when he was convicted (temporarily, for the conviction was overturned) in a financial dispute surrounding the canal, so unfortunately he had no participation in the ultimate canal design.

Other examples of Eiffel's work can be seen in his homeland. In 1900 he was the primary designer for the Parisian La Ruche, a building that served originally as a wine rotunda but was later repurposed as housing for artists. He also created a hallmark dome on the Nice Observatory, a building completed in 1888 in Nice, France. This observatory housed what was, at the time,

The Statue of Liberty was built in Paris before being shipped across the Atlantic Ocean to its home in New York City. This photograph shows the statue enclosed by scaffolding while it was under construction in 1884.

the largest telescope in the world.

Toward the end of his life, Eiffel became more interested in flight and aerodynamics. He designed and constructed a laboratory for aerodynamics, and he used the Eiffel Tower as a testing ground for several of his interests, including radio broadcasting tools and a wind tunnel. Eiffel died in Paris in 1923.

THE STATUE OF LIBERTY

Another one of Alexandre-Gustave Eiffel's famous projects was the Statue of Liberty. This massive statue, now a New York City landmark, was given by France to the United States in 1885. It was placed on Liberty Island in the Hudson River and was intended to welcome immigrants into the country. It was engineered by Eiffel and sculpted under the direction of Auguste Bartholdi.

Eiffel's major contribution was the creation of the iron sub-skeleton upon which the copper skin was placed. The skeleton used four major posts that were under compression from a secondary skeleton; the lattice-shaped connecting bars were attached to this second frame. Two smaller skeletons branched off the main body, one to shape the head and the other to hold the torch arm. The framework Eiffel designed was not unlike that of the steel-framed skyscrapers that would be built in the years to come.

FAMOUS COPIES

There have been several other tall steel or iron towers built in the style and form of the Eiffel Tower. One modern imitator is the Kiev television tower in the Ukraine. Built in 1973, the Kiev tower reaches a height of 1,263 feet (385 meters). It is one of the tallest metal structures in the world and, while more modernistic in appearance than the Eiffel Tower, it is clearly based on the same design. The base has four legs and is built completely from steel tubes. Unlike the Eiffel Tower, which was riveted together, the Kiev tower's connections are welded.

Another well-known Eiffel look-alike is the Crystal Palace transmitting station in South London. It stands 728 feet (222 meters) tall. Sometimes

ACHIEVEMENT IN IRON

Numerous copies have been made of the Eiffel Tower; this version was built in Tokyo, Japan.

called the Eiffel Tower of London, the Crystal Palace transmits both UHF (ultra high frequency) and VHF (very high frequency) television signals, in addition to digital television and radio.

The Eiffel Tower tells a very powerful story, one of innovation, technology, and achievement. Its success paved the way for future innovations in steel, and many subsequent projects took advantage of the advances made by the Eiffel Tower team. One example is the St. Louis Gateway Arch, a massive stainless steel structure that again challenged existing notions of what a metal structure could do.

Miracle of Glass: Louvre Pyramid

Metal and glass make a striking combination, especially when used on a large scale. The Louvre pyramid, designed by architect I.M. Pei for the Louvre, France's national museum and art gallery, was built in 1989 and serves as the entrance to the museum's catacombs. It stands out in direct contrast to the main building, which was originally built in 1535. The French president at the time the pyramid was designed, Francois Mitterrand, specifically requested that this entrance reflect technology and modernization.

Generally speaking, pyramids are structurally sound shapes. A pyramid is a type of polyhedron, or multisided shape, consisting of a base and faces that meet at the top to form the apex. A tetrahedron, composed of four triangular faces, consists of a triangular base and three sides.

The glass pyramid constructed at the entrance of the Louvre museum in Paris presents a study in contrasts between modern and traditional architecture.

Architect I.M. Pei used repeating triangles and diamonds of glass and metal to construct the pyramid. His choice of materials sparked controversy initially, due to the aesthetic contrast with the existing traditional façade of the Louvre.

A square pyramid has a square base with triangular sides.

The Louvre pyramid was designed as a series of four interconnected glass pyramids, including one main square pyramid and three smaller ones. It reaches a maximum height of about 70 feet (20.5 meters) and contains more than 670 separate glass panes. The structure acts as a skylight, allowing light to come into both the pyramid and the Louvre entrance.

The glass panes are held in place by a steel structure combined with steel tensioning cables. The panes, designed by Saint-Gobain, a French company that fabricates glass, plastics, and other polymers, contain a special reflective coating. The panes vary in shape, though most are diamond-shaped or triangular. The pyramid has a tessellated, faceted appearance, which contributes to a grand overall effect.

Pei's design was controversial, as many critics argued that the modernistic design clashed uncomfortably with the traditional exterior of the rest of the Louvre. However, like many innovative designs (including the Eiffel Tower), the Louvre pyramid is now an accepted part of the architecture of Paris and an integral part of the Louvre itself.

CHAPTER 2

CELEBRATION OF EXPANSION

The St. Louis Gateway Arch

The idea of a city building a gargantuan arch, either for function or for personal acclaim, is not a new one. Roman aqueducts were huge arched structures that carried water to surrounding areas. These arches were both useful and beautiful, showing the Roman commitment to careful and aesthetic design.

Other early arches were purely for show. Roman emperors had elaborately sculpted stone arches built to commemorate their lives and military achievements. These appeared throughout the Roman territories and were later copied by European rulers during the Renaissance.

Self-promotion was extremely important in the early days of Western European civilization, but became less so with the advent of democracy. The St. Louis Gateway Arch in Missouri is a grand example of a modern arch that was constructed to commemorate the glory of a nation rather than an individual.

The city of St. Louis was founded in the eighteenth century by fur traders from France, when the region was still part of Spanish territory. The city was named in honor of the French king, Louis IX. The city was

Arches were used as stable building types in ancient times. One example is this aqueduct built in 19 B.C.E. by the Romans in Languedoc, France.

MODERN WONDERS

retroceded to France in 1800 and in 1803 was acquired by the United States as part of the Louisiana Purchase.

The Lewis and Clark Expedition set out from St. Louis in 1804, sent by President Thomas Jefferson to explore the Pacific Northwest. This event and the great move westward, during which many Americans passed through St. Louis, led to the city's nickname, "Gateway to the West."

A grand arch was conceived in the 1940s and built in the 1960s as a way of celebrating President Jefferson, St. Louis, and the city's role in the opening of the West. Today the Gateway Arch, together with the courthouse and the Museum of Westward Expansion, form the Jefferson National Expansion Memorial, which is part of the U.S. National Park Service.

THE ARCHITECT

Eero Saarinen (1910–1961) was the mastermind behind the Gateway Arch. Saarinen was a Finnish architect who studied in the United States and became known for his organic, curving forms. One of the most famous

Arches were heavily used in architect Eero Saarinen's design of the TWA Terminal at John F. Kennedy International Airport in New York, shown under construction in 1961.

examples of this style is the TWA Terminal at John F. Kennedy International Airport in New York, which has several large, leaf-like structures emanating from its center.

The St. Louis arch was one of Saarinen's first major works without the collaboration of his architect father, Eliel. The younger Saarinen won a design competition in 1947 for this project. His design was meant as a tribute to Thomas Jefferson and St. Louis, as well as a celebration of technology and the modern era. The main engineer for the arch was Fred Severud (1899–1990), a Norwegian civil engineer who worked with Saarinen on several other projects. Severud's major contribution to the project was his technological and engineering expertise, knowledge that went into the arch's height and stability.

Structural Design

The Gateway Arch is an imposing structure, measuring 630 feet (192 meters) tall and 630 feet (192 meters) wide at the base. Its materials weigh over 43,000 tons! The foundations for the arch each measure about 60 feet (18 meters) high, which is about one-tenth of the overall height of the arch. Approximately half of each reinforced concrete foundation is buried in bedrock, creating a very stable base for the arch.

The foundations were tensioned using steel bars because, while concrete has excellent strength in compression, it requires the additional tensile strength of steel to form a material that excels in both tension and compression. The steel in the foundations was prestressed, meaning it had artificial loads applied to it so that when placed into position and under the actual material loads, the steel would bend slightly and compress into the proper position. These steel tensioning bars eventually had to curve into the proper shape to fit the curvature of the arch. Prestressing ensured that when segments of the arch were built upon this foundation, the steel would not bend out of position and lose strength.

Because it would have been impossible to create the arch out of one continuous piece of steel, it was built in segments. Each piece measured 12 feet (3.5 meters) wide at the bottom of each leg and narrowed as it reached the top of the arch. Each segment of the arch legs uses a

MODERN WONDERS

The Gateway Arch, in St. Louis, Missouri, makes an unforgettable addition to the city skyline.

construction method called double-wall, meaning each section of the arch actually has two layers of steel. Since the legs of the arch had to be left hollow in order for people to be transported up to the top of the arch, it was not possible to design an interior steel skeleton that took up a lot of space. The double-wall design essentially allowed for two structures, one inside the other, which created a very strong and durable design.

Most of Gateway Arch's sections were partially assembled off-site, then welded and bolted together in position at the construction site. Cranes assisted in the construction up to a point and—as in the construction of the Eiffel Tower—when the structure reached a height that exceeded what the regular cranes could reach, creeper cranes walked up the legs of the arch

CELEBRATION OF EXPANSION

The Gateway Arch under construction in 1965.

27

MODERN WONDERS

> ### STABILIZING TRUSS
>
> The Gateway Arch required the addition of an extra truss during construction. The arch was built "legs first." The legs were built in segments that arched toward each other, and the middle gap was bridged at the top with the keystone arch segments. Prior to constructing these all-important middle segments, the design team had a serious issue to face: once the arched legs were built to about 530 feet (161 meters) tall, the legs were leaning inward to the point where they could have become unstable and collapsed. To solve this problem, a massive steel truss was built and raised into position. Its purpose was to provide temporary support for the legs while they awaited the construction of the keystone portions of the arch. The truss was connected to each leg of the arch and served to brace the arch legs, preventing any unwanted movement or deflection. Once the arch was finished, the truss was removed.

to attach the triangular segments together. These creepers each weighed about 100 tons and were custom built to climb the legs of the arch.

How did workers manage to get to the upper levels of the arch to connect the segments together? A temporary elevator was erected on site to transport workers up to the level of the crane, which placed the heavy triangular segments into the correct locations. The elevator was designed to use the same tracks as the creeper cranes, but it had a mechanism inside to keep the elevator car level at all times.

Exterior

The arch is built of stainless steel, giving it a shiny, mirrored appearance. The cross-section of the base legs forms an equilateral triangle, or a triangle with three equal sides. Each side measures 54 feet (16 meters) wide at the bottom of the arch, and each triangle tapers to measure 17 feet

The Gateway Arch's trademark design elements include carefully calculated curvatures and highly reflective surfaces.

(5 meters) per side at the very top of the arch.

The exterior walls were made of stainless steel, which is a high-grade steel with a low carbon content. In order to be called stainless steel, the metal must contain at least 10 percent chromium. When first exposed to oxygen, the chromium in the stainless steel forms a layer of chromium oxide that gives the metal its perpetually shiny appearance. Another convenient property of stainless steel is that it does not rust; this is very useful for a gigantic steel arch that could not be easily polished from the outside.

Each exterior panel was highly polished and bolted in sections to the interior wall, which was made of carbon steel. This iron-steel alloy comes in different combinations of carbon and iron. More carbon makes the steel very strong but also less flexible and more difficult to weld. Less carbon creates more ductile steel that is easier to work with but is less strong.

The overall thickness of each interior steel section was 3/8 inch (1 centimeter), but the corners were five times this thickness. This extra material at the corners made the structure more resistant to bending from the internal and external loads acting on the arch. Bending occurs when an object is subjected to forces that cause it to deflect. A horizontal beam

ALLOWING FOR BENDING

How did the engineers know how thick to make the corners of the Gateway Arch? The calculations for what it would take to cause steel to bend can be seen as a combination of the loads acting upon the steel times the length of the steel segment. The maximum amount of bending that a particular structural element might be likely to experience can also be determined by multiplying the section modulus (a value that comes from the dimensions of the steel section) by the maximum bending stress of the steel (a value that comes from the steel manufacturer). By calculating these values, the engineers determined how much to increase the corner thickness in order to prevent possible problems with bending, such as weakening of the material and even potential breakage.

supported at either end might bend, for example, when too much weight is placed in the middle of the beam.

The Curve

The overall shape of the arch is a particular type of curve, called an inverted *catenary*. A catenary curve is the name for the shape that is formed when a chain, such as a necklace, is held at two points and allowed to droop in the center. The only force acting on a catenary is its own weight under the force of gravity. Saarinen designed the Gateway Arch as an inverted catenary, or a catenary curve that was flipped upside down.

Catenary curves are just one of many kinds of curves. A similar curve is the *parabola*, which has a slightly different shape and a different mathematical equation. Catenary and parabola curves are similar in appearance and are both symmetrical. Their mathematical equations are:

CELEBRATION OF EXPANSION

Parabola: $y = a x^2 + b x + c$

Catenary: $y = a \cosh\left(\dfrac{x}{a}\right) = \dfrac{a}{2}(e^{x/a} + e^{-x/a})$

The parabola is a simple curve that is a type of conic section and is defined geometrically as the intersection of a cone and a plane in which the plane is parallel to the surface of the cone. Any particular value of y, which is the location of a point in the vertical direction, can be found by taking x, the value in the horizontal direction, and applying the above equation to it: a, b, and c are constants that govern the location and size of the parabola.

A catenary curve has a more complicated equation. It involves the function *cosh*, which is the hyperbolic cosine function. Cosh is similar to the more familiar cosine function, but while cosine and sine are based on a circle, cosh and its counterpart *sinh* are based on a hyperbola. A catenary curve is one of the more common applications of hyperbolic functions, but its equation can also be expressed in exponential form by using the irrational number e.

In the equation for the catenary curve above, the constant a is defined as (T/P), where T is the horizontal component of the tension force, and

One of the most unique aspects of the Gateway Arch is its geometrical form. It is shaped like an upside-down catenary curve (pink), which is similar to the more common parabola (blue).

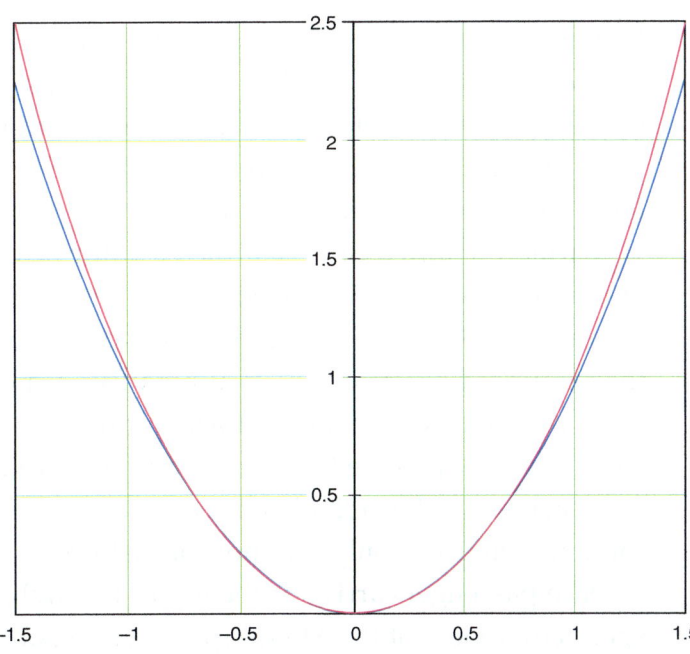

31

P is the weight of the hanging chain per unit of length. The exact formula for the Gateway Arch is:

$$y = -127.7 \text{ ft } \cosh(x/127.7 \text{ ft}) + 757.7 \text{ ft}$$

So why did Saarinen choose a catenary instead of a parabola for the shape of the Gateway Arch? The answer lies mainly in the physical properties of the shapes. The catenary curve, when hung from two points, fully supports its own weight as long as the two ends are properly supported. The inverse property is also true; if the catenary is inverted, as in the arch, it is able to support its own weight provided the ends are sufficiently well anchored. The steep slope of the catenary curve near the ends allows most of the forces on the arch to be guided downward into the foundation, with very little force transferred laterally. The nature of the parabola, which is wider at the ends, is that it does not maintain this particular shape without additional reinforcement. In other words, it would deform slightly under its own weight and would be a poor choice for a large structure.

TRAM TO THE TOP

Visitors today can access the top of the Gateway Arch via a tram that climbs its way up the inside of the arch's legs. The system was conceived by Dick Bowser, an elevator designer who happened to be in the right place at the right time and convinced Eero Saarinen that he could formulate a plan for the arch's elevator system.

Saarinen required only that the elevator be completely concealed by the arch, and that it could transport from 430 to 780 people per hour up and down the arch. The design Bowser produced involved capsules, rather than standard elevator cars, that held five seated people each. Eight capsules were linked together to form a train, and the capsules step and rotate their way to the top of the arch in a trip that takes about four minutes each way. The arch also has a set of stairs (over 1,000 steps!) that is for emergency use only and not for visitors.

Once passengers arrive at the top of the arch, they are rewarded with a spectacular view of the Mississippi River. Visibility can stretch about

CELEBRATION OF EXPANSION

30 miles (49 kilometers), depending on the weather conditions. The view more than makes up for the cramped quarters at the top of the arch and the tiny windows that allow the observation chamber to remain almost invisible from the ground.

More Arches Around the World

One of the world's largest commemorative arches is the Arc de Triomphe in Paris. The arch was originally commissioned by Napoleon I in 1806, but was not completed until thirty years later. It is part of a series of monuments at the Place Charles de Gaulle.

The triumphal arch was often used in ancient times to celebrate military victories, as in the Arc de Triomphe in Paris. This arch was commissioned by Napoleon I in 1806.

MODERN WONDERS

The Arc de Triomphe was designed in the tradition of the Roman triumphal arch from the first century C.E., but on quite a grand scale at 164 feet (50 meters) tall. The arch is elaborately decorated with friezes, or horizontal bands of sculpture. It was intended to commemorate Napoleon's military victories. The final design of the arch is an homage to the French army during this period.

The arch shape is repeated in the Arche de la Défense, an office building near Paris.

CELEBRATION OF EXPANSION

A completely different type of arch is the Arche de la Défense, located near Paris. This mammoth arch was designed by Johann Otto von Spreckelsen and finished in 1989. It is actually nearly square in shape with a total height of 360 feet (110 meters). The competition to design the arch was set in motion by President Francois Mitterrand, who wanted to make an arch suitable for modern France. Post-tensioned steel and concrete were used to create the structure, and massive concrete piers form the foundation. The exterior is clad with marble and granite.

Unlike triumphal arches from the Roman period, the Arche de la Defénse is an homage to the city and also a usable space. Thirty-seven stories of office buildings are located in the arch's legs. The Arc de Triomphe and the Arche de la Defénse differ in both form and purpose from the St. Louis Gateway Arch, but all three are good examples of how societies have used arches in their memorial architecture.

One way to create a lasting impression is to produce something original, the likes of which has never been seen before. The St. Louis Gateway Arch meets the criteria, and many later structures also stand out by virtue of the creativity, originality, and technical prowess that went into their creation.

Following in the tradition of this magnificent arch, the art of curvilinear architecture that developed in subsequent years is quickly becoming the future of architectural design.

CHAPTER
3

CURVILINEAR DESIGN

Curvilinear design is the art and science of creating structures and objects out of curving forms. This fantastically exciting field is new, having been developed only in the last few decades as computers became powerful enough to model the cutting-edge designs. The antithesis of the curvilinear building—the "straight" building—has been around since time began; post-and-beam construction is one of the oldest forms of architecture and has been utilized and improved on for generations. It is important to understand this basic technique in order to appreciate the differences in the new curvilinear style.

LINES AND CURVES

The roof ribs and panels of the Sydney Opera House, in New South Wales, Australia, were constructed on-site in prefabricated units.

Successful post-and-beam buildings can be made of various natural materials, such as stone and wood, and are fairly simple to construct. Small structures can be built using this method without heavy machinery or large numbers of workers. These buildings also have a clear structural diagram, making them easy to understand and replicate. Vertical posts support the horizontal beams, which in turn support loads from the rest of the structure. Intermediate vertical posts are often used to provide a structure for the cladding.

37

The structural diagram of post-and-beam construction is quite simple: vertical posts support a horizontal column that contains both tension and compression.

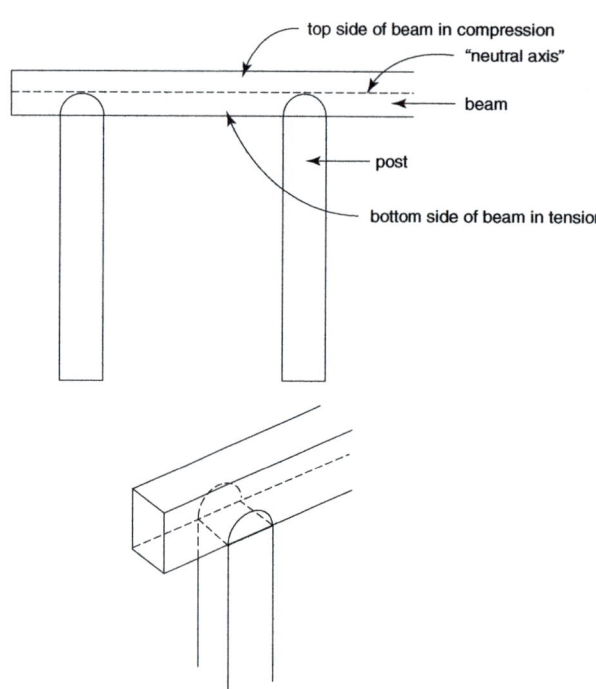

While post-and-beam buildings tend to be square or rectangular, many ancient societies used variations on this structural system to create round buildings. The Pantheon in Rome, for example, has a grand circular rotunda that is today one of the best examples of Roman engineering. The Pantheon curves in only one direction, however. It is more difficult to construct a building that curves in different directions at the same time.

To illustrate the concept of curving in different directions, take a piece of paper and wrap it into a cylinder. In doing this, the paper curves in one direction (the x plane). Now take the cylinder and slowly bend it to one side, as if forming half of a rainbow. The paper is now curving in two directions (x and y planes). Circular buildings that curve in a single direction are, from a structural point of view, fairly easy to construct because loads from the building materials are still acting straight down. Buildings that curve in different directions, on the other hand, are considerably more difficult to design, document, engineer, and construct.

Construction Documentation

Construction documents include drawings that detail every aspect of the building and how it should be built. When architecture was confined to simple wooden or stone buildings, it was probably sufficient for an engineer to specify a basic layout using whatever means were available. To construct a modern house, library, or office building, however, fully

CURVILINEAR DESIGN

detailed construction documents are required. In the past, these drawings were done by hand using traditional architectural tools for drawing straight lines and right angles. Drafting triangles, parallel edge bars, and templates with predefined cutout shapes were the most common tools used for drafting a building plan.

Toward the end of the twentieth century, a significant invention opened an entirely new world to architects: the computer, along with software for designing three-dimensional objects. In addition to revolutionizing most aspects of society, computers provided a special boon to architects because of the development of design and drafting software. With this new tool, designing three-dimensional curved surfaces became nearly effortless, and the buildings produced by cutting-edge architects fully demonstrate these new capabilities.

JORN UTZON

One of the most distinctive Australian works of architecture, the Sydney Opera House, was designed before the advent of computer-aided design software. It is important to a discussion on designs using

The Sydney Opera House of 1973 is a modern expressionist performance theater that uses an innovative shell design, combining beauty with acoustical excellence.

39

MODERN WONDERS

this technology, however, because it was one of the first large-scale buildings to be designed using bold curvilinear forms. The Opera House was designed toward the end of the modern period.

Modernism was a trend in culture, art, and architecture that occurred in the early 1900s, lasting until about 1945. During this period, new styles and colors were used to create an appearance distinctive from the styles of the past. Toward the end of the modern period, architects began creating works that were identified more by the style of the architect and less by the period (the end of which was loosely dubbed expressionist). The Sydney Opera House did not reflect any particular overarching style of the day but rather the genius of Jorn Utzon, its designer.

More than 67,800 square feet (6,300 square meters) of glass were used for the Sydney Opera House facades.

CURVILINEAR DESIGN

DECONSTRUCTIONISM

The philosophical movement called desconstructionism emerged in the 1960s. Led by the French philosopher Jacques Derrida, deconstructionists interpreted philosophy and literature by breaking down individual paragraphs, lines, and phrases into their composite elements. In doing so, it was thought that the true meaning of such works might be discovered.

In the 1980s, this type of analysis was applied to a wide range of disciplines, from the law to film and architecture. Deconstructionist buildings were physically fragmented and altered. The logic of a traditional building was turned upside down, and the resulting architecture took on a drastically new appearance.

Peter Eisenman (b. 1932) is generally considered to be a central architect of the deconstructionist movement. The Wexner Center at Ohio State University is an Eisenman design that is constructed from concrete, steel, and glass. It contains what is known as a "shifted grid," or intersecting grids. These grids are one of the hallmarks of Eisenman's style and, in this case, they help to direct traffic flow in and out of the building.

Another major architect of the deconstructionist style is Zaha Hadid (b. 1950). Her projects, such as the Rosenthal Center for Contemporary Art in Cincinnati and the Vitra Fire Station in Germany, incorporate sharp, protruding angles. These angular components make the buildings appear fragmented, as if they were made of many pieces rather than being one distinct whole; this is one of several ways in which deconstructionism has been interpreted by architects around the world.

The Rosenthal Center for Contemporary Art in Cincinnati, Ohio, uses a combination of materials and geometry to form a design that resembles a 3-D puzzle.

Jorn Utzon (b. 1918) is a Danish architect who became known for his design of private homes. Utzon won the commission of the Opera House as a result of an international competition. Over the course of this project, Utzon refined his skills for designing shells, or complex shapes that are derived from a basic spherical form. The Opera House took fourteen years to build (1959–1973) and required several stages of construction.

The building occupies more than four acres at Bennelong Point and measures 600 feet (183 meters) by 385 feet (120 meters). The complex contains five separate concert halls and nearly 1,000 other rooms. It was designed as a connected series of elliptical shells. While the original design did not call for the vaults that are apparent in the structure, the smoother surfaces Utzon had in mind proved too difficult to construct. A design compromise was therefore made in conjunction with the engineering firm responsible for the project, Ove Arup and Partners. The curving, fluid shells have a particularly organic feel and also contribute to the acoustic properties of the music theaters.

The roof shells were constructed of precast concrete. Each roof shell is actually a double shell. The two outer shells are connected by a rib-like interior structure. The shells were cast in sections and attached to the main building structure using pretensioned steel cables. Large concrete columns provide the basic structural support for the roofs. The largest column measures about 8 feet (2.5 meters) by 8 feet (2.5 meters). The roof is covered with a layer of Swedish ceramic tiles, and interior surfaces are lined with native granite and wood.

Due to some unfortunate political squabbling, Utzon was fired from the project before construction was completed. At the time of his dismissal, construction was running nearly a year behind schedule and had far exceeded the budget.

The Sydney Opera House was ahead of its time in terms of design and engineering, and it remains today one of the most magnificent examples of curvilinear design anywhere in the world.

FRANK GEHRY

Perhaps the quintessential "curvy" modern architect is Frank Gehry (b. 1929). Arguably as much sculptor as architect, Gehry has designed

CURVILINEAR DESIGN

Architect Frank Gehry made extensive use of computer modeling software in both the design and construction phases of the Guggenheim Museum built in Bilbao in 1997.

numerous buildings and residences that display his characteristic method of design. The major hallmarks of his style include curvilinear forms that do not fit neatly into a rectangular space, protruding elements, and brightly reflective metal exteriors. He is based in Los Angeles, California, and has worked all over the world.

Guggenheim Museum, Bilbao, Spain

One of Gehry's signature projects is the Guggenheim Museum in Bilbao, Spain. Gehry makes extensive use of advanced computer-aided design software when conceptualizing his buildings, and this project in particular could not have been completed without the aid of special software that helped the fabricators produce the pieces correctly. Completed in 1997, this modern art museum is a highly stylized tribute to a fish, an appropriate gesture given that Bilbao is a port city.

While the rectilinear portions of the museum were constructed in limestone, the more fluid portions were built using a steel frame covered with titanium and glass. Steel was selected primarily because it excels in tension; the odd angles of some of the protruding elements in this building caused extra tension forces to act upon the structure. In a typical rectilinear post-and-beam structure, supporting columns are placed in compression because the loads acting down on them are vertical. But when the loads come from a variety of angles, as is found in a complex curved structure, both tension and compression forces may be present, and so materials must be used that can withstand both types of force.

Walt Disney Concert Hall

Another example of Gehry's work in curvilinear design is the Walt Disney Concert Hall in Los Angeles, California. Occupying 293,000 square feet (27,000 square meters), the hall was designed primarily for the Los Angeles Philharmonic and was the result of a design competition. In addition to a main auditorium, important parts of the complex include an elaborate lobby space, gardens, and outdoor performance spaces. Construction was delayed several times and ultimately took sixteen years. The building opened to the public in 2003.

The building is an organic combination of different shapes with the auditorium as the definitive focus. The interior is lined with different types of wood, including cedar and fir, which give the building a warm feel. In contrast, the exterior is clad in stainless steel panels, which are striking in appearance. More than 6,000 panels were used in the cladding. Due to the nature of the curvature of the building's surfaces, the majority were custom sizes and could not be mass-produced. Thick glass skylights allow natural light to flow into the interior spaces.

In an interesting design decision, Gehry omitted separate seating areas, generally called boxes, which are often reserved for those who purchase higher-priced tickets. The priority in the interior design was the acoustics. Equal sounds were to be reflected into all parts of the main seating area. One of the major structural factors that helped with the acoustics was the convex curvature of the upper panels; these allowed sound waves to

SPECULAR REFLECTION

Some may like it hot, but how about sizzling hot? When construction of the Walt Disney Concert Hall's steel exterior was initially completed, residents of nearby apartments complained that they were getting excessive glare and heat through their windows. As it turned out, sunlight was reflecting off the shiny surface of the building and straight into their apartments. This was the result of a specular reflection, which refers to a beam of light encountering a reflective surface and then bouncing off that surface in a single direction.

When light hits most objects, it bounces off the surface and is scattered in multiple directions. This scattering effect, referred to as diffuse reflection, reduces the intensity of the light that is reflected in any one particular direction. But when light hits a highly polished surface, such as a mirror, the beam of light is not scattered and instead is reflected in a particular direction.

The law of reflection governs the relationship between the incidence and reflectance angles, and simply states that θ_i[CBP1] $= \theta_r$, where θ_i is the incidence angle as measured with respect to the surface normal (a line at a right angle to the surface), and θ_r is the reflectance angle as measured with respect to the surface normal.

The steel plates initially installed on the Walt Disney Concert Hall were so highly polished that they allowed a specular reflection to bounce sunlight into certain buildings nearby. To counteract this glare, problematic surfaces on the building had to be sanded so that they became less reflective, resulting in more diffuse reflection of incident sunlight.

When a ray of light intersects a reflective surface, it bounces off the surface at a right angle.

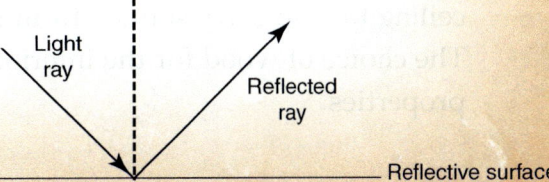

MODERN WONDERS

The Disney Concert Hall—designed by Frank Gehry in 1987, with construction completed in 2003—contains a mix of stone and metal facades, with a natural wood interior.

bounce off them and back down into the auditorium, providing a very full and rich aural experience.

A separate company, Nagata Acoustics, helped to design the main auditorium. The design included elements such as a suspended wooden ceiling to help carry sounds from the stage to all parts of the auditorium. The choice of wood for the interior also enhances the space's acoustic properties.

Wood's Acoustic Properties

Why was wood the chosen material for the concert hall? Consider a stringed musical instrument, such as the violin. When a player rubs the violin strings with a bow, the string vibrates against the bridge of the violin, which transfers that vibration into the violin's wooden body. The body's vibrations make the air inside and around the violin vibrate. This air disturbance is the audible sound wave heard when the violin is played. The notes that are heard depend on the tension of the string (controlled by the tuning pegs as well as by the player's fingers on a given string) and the size and shape of the instrument.

A sound wave is a vibrational wave that has a particular frequency, or period of oscillation. The higher the frequency, the higher the pitch of the sound wave. Frequency is inversely related to wavelength—the higher the frequency, the shorter the wavelength. A string bass is a large instrument that produces long-wavelength sounds that are low in pitch. A smaller instrument, such as a violin, will produce short-wavelength sounds that are high in pitch.

Wood is a resonant material, which means that it vibrates easily when exposed to sound waves. Sound waves travel faster through less dense materials, and stringed instruments are therefore made of wood because it allows the sound waves to propagate and be amplified naturally by the shape of the interior cavity. Metal, on the other hand, is highly dense and, on its own, does not resonate as wood does. In buildings, wooden interiors provide a good acoustic environment precisely because of this resonant quality, which helps to naturally propagate and amplify the music being played.

New Materials

The future of curvilinear design depends, in large part, on the availability of computer software that can keep up with the imaginations of designers. It also depends on materials that can be easily formed into any conceivable shape.

Titanium and Bendable Concrete

Titanium is an extremely strong material that makes an excellent cladding for buildings. It is lightweight and has a low modulus of elasticity, which is a measurement that determines a material's tendency to deform. Modulus of elasticity (λ) is defined as stress (the force causing a deformation, or bending) divided by strain (how much the object has deviated from its original shape):

$$\lambda = stress/strain$$

Titanium's low modulus means it is quite flexible and can easily be manufactured into curved surfaces. This flexibility also makes it an excellent choice for use in earthquake-prone regions.

Another new building material that holds great promise for the designs of the future is bendable concrete. Rather than being reinforced with traditional steel bars, this new type of concrete has a greater tension capability from the addition of flexible fiber reinforcements. These polypropylene or carbon fibers make the concrete 500 times more flexible than traditional concrete and therefore much less likely to crack during bending. Bendable concrete is useful in constructing bridges and roads, as well as buildings.

Translucent Materials

Translucent concrete can add a unique element to a building's lighting design. This special type of concrete is embedded with optical glass fibers. Light passes from one side of the concrete through to the other side, making the concrete units translucent.

Some amount of light passes through translucent objects, but not enough so that the object is transparent (like glass). A transparent object allows light to pass right through it, giving a clear view of objects on the other side. A translucent material, on the other hand, absorbs and scatters some of the incident light. It still allows some of the light to pass through the object, but the resulting image is fuzzy or distorted. Depending on the degree of translucence, the object may just allow ambient light to pass without producing an image. A clear glass window is transparent, whereas a frosted glass window is translucent.

Translucent concrete has the ability to brighten the interiors of concrete buildings, which tend to be dark since regular concrete does not transmit light. This new material presents new potential for the use of concrete in many different situations.

Innovations in architecture and technology are constantly being made. Another, somewhat fanciful building material that is being explored is ice. Hotels made of ice are part of a new wave of architectural design that breaks away from the conventions of traditional architecture.

CHAPTER 4

WORKING COLD

Architecture on Ice

Most discussions on architecture are concerned with traditional buildings of brick, stone, wood, or some other conventional material. But some architecture worth learning about is designed to be operational for a limited period of time.

One example of a transient structure is a military hospital. They can be assembled in just a few hours and disassembled in an even shorter period of time, yet they are fully functional architecture that can house everything from offices to full surgical suites. Tents are temporary structures that meet the occupants' basic need of protection from the elements and are erected for a number of purposes: a store's "tent sale," a wedding, or some other outdoor event. Some tents are even climate-controlled. Full-scale models of Santa's village that are set up in shopping malls around the United States every December are another example of seasonal architecture.

These examples consist of temporary architecture that can be assembled very quickly. There are limits to this type of architecture. Most are not aesthetically appealing and cannot accommodate grand architectural gestures. While functional, these structures are not particularly interesting or inspiring. An exception to this is the ice hotel. There are only a few ice hotels in the world at any given time, constructed in locations cold enough to keep them frozen throughout the winter months.

The Jukkasjärvi Ice Hotel, located in Sweden, is completely rebuilt each year from ice and snow.

PROPERTIES OF ICE

Ice is a distinct solid with specific intrinsic properties. Water, like all other types of matter, comes in three basic states: solid, liquid, and gas. In its liquid state, water flows in rain and rivers, faucets and garden hoses. Gaseous water, or water vapor, occurs when water evaporates and becomes steam or clouds. Solid water results when water freezes to a temperate below 32 degrees Fahrenheit (0 degrees Celsius), and it includes ice, hail, and snow.

The definition of a solid is a rigid material with a finite volume. Solids hold their shape until some external energy input forces a phase change, or forces it to change into a liquid or gas. Heat is one of those inputs; expose ice to heat, and it will turn back into water and then steam.

In the days before refrigeration, ice was taken from cold regions and stored in temperature-resistant spaces. It was also used in early air-conditioning systems. Ice is used as a preservative in the food and medical industries, and it forms the basis for winter sports such as ice hockey, bobsled racing, and curling.

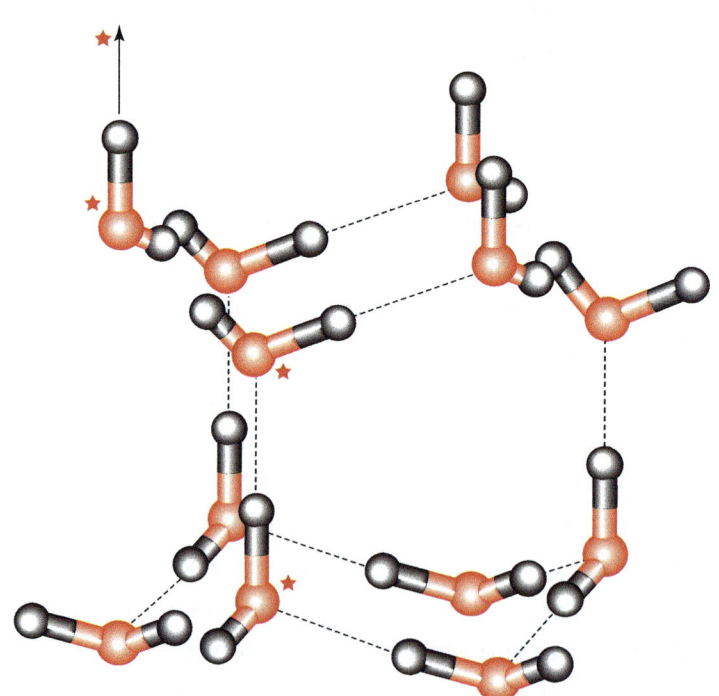

Ice forms a crystalline lattice in which each oxygen atom (the red circles) is accompanied by two hydrogen atoms (the gray sticks). The hydrogen atoms stick together with a strong bond called a hydrogen bond, forming a hexagonal structure.

52

DRY ICE

Dry ice is frozen carbon dioxide (CO_2), the gas that mammals exhale while breathing out. Carbon dioxide can undergo a phase change directly from solid to gas, bypassing the liquid phase. This process is called sublimation.

Dry ice exists at very cold temperatures, around −109°F (−78°C) and cannot be touched with bare hands. Dry ice is produced from liquid CO_2 that is usually contained in high-pressure containers. When allowed to enter a space with normal atmospheric pressure, the liquid CO_2 turns into gas; the sudden change in phase results in a large temperature drop of the material. While some of the gas evaporates, the rest freezes into a powdery form of dry ice, which is then compressed into solid dry ice.

Ice is a crystalline solid. While the crystals can come in twelve different shapes, the most common types of ice crystals are made up of a hexagonal lattice, a lattice structure with six sides. An interesting fact about ice is that it floats in liquid water. Most substances become denser and tend to sink when they change phase from liquid to solid and are placed in a liquid. But water becomes less dense when it freezes. Ice's crystalline structure expands the volume of the ice, which in turn decreases the density. Water is the only nonmetallic substance that is lighter as a solid than it is as a liquid.

IGLOOS

Igloos and snow houses have been the traditional dwellings in arctic areas for at least hundreds of years and perhaps much longer. They are commonly constructed by the Inuit, the indigenous inhabitants of Siberia, Alaska, Greenland, and parts of Canada.

MODERN WONDERS

Native people in northern cultures built igloos from blocks of compressed snow. Snow is a good insulator, allowing temperatures inside to be warm even on extremely cold days or nights.

Igloos are built from compacted snow. When it is wind-blown or pressed into solid blocks by hand, the loose crystalline structure of snow changes into ice. Ice is denser and easier to work with than snow. Blocks are carved and stacked, usually to form a dome-like shape. The blocks are leaned into one another in such a way that tension and compression forces are balanced out. Because these forces are in equilibrium, no internal structure is required for the dome to maintain its shape. As in the construction of an arch, the uppermost blocks of the igloo are carved into keystone shapes, and then wedged into position. Finally, the dome's surfaces are polished to remove any harsh edges.

Igloo inhabitants use lamps inside. The heat from these lamps slightly melts the interior of the dome, but once the lamp is turned off the melted portion refreezes. A thin sheet of ice forms on the interior surface of the dome, and this layer contributes to the igloo's structural integrity.

A few basic tools are all that is needed to build an igloo: gloves, or something to protect the worker's hands from the freezing temperatures; some type of saw or cutting device to hew the blocks of frozen snow; and a shovel or scoop for removing the upper layers of unpacked snow that cover the higher-density snow and ice layers used for building.

Ice must be kept below the freezing temperature of water, so how do people survive inside an ice structure? Snow is a terrific insulator. Because of its lattice structure, most of the volume in a mass of lightly packed snow is actually air. Air, on its own, does not support the transfer of heat from one location to another, so in the absence of high winds or other external forces, snow will provide a successful barrier between freezing outside temperatures and more habitable indoor temperatures.

ICE HOTEL JUKKASJÄRVI

Igloos are a common sight in several parts of the world, but they are exotic and intriguing structures to people who have never seen them up close. The novelty of ice structures makes them a tremendous tourist attraction, and so a new architectural typology has sprung forth in recent years: the ice hotel.

The first large commercial ice hotel was created in the village of Jukkasjärvi, Sweden. Every winter, a new hotel is built using ice from the frozen Torne River. Once the region warms up to the point where the ice

The Jukkasjärvi Ice Hotel is built from 10,000 tons of ice and 30,000 tons of snow.

MODERN WONDERS

The Ice Hotel contains around eighty bedrooms, as well as a bar, movie theater, and chapel (seen here).

begins to melt, the ice is returned to the river. The concept for the ice hotel began with an igloo. In 1990 a French artist named Jannot Derit presented an art show in an igloo built on the frozen Torne River. Later, a group of travelers brought sleeping bags and spent the night inside the igloo. After they bragged about how well they slept in the igloo, the idea for the hotel began to take shape.

The area of the hotel and associated chapel totals about 64,000 square feet (6,000 square meters.) The hotel currently offers eighty guest rooms, and is open December through April. One of the most interesting aspects of the ice hotel is that it is designed in a different configuration each year. This is one of the great luxuries of rebuilding the site on a seasonal basis! New ideas in art and architecture are incorporated into each year's hotel, which is crafted by snow builders over several months. Because the water in the Torne River is fast-flowing, the ice used in the hotel is especially clear and makes for a gorgeous, crystalline building.

Beds and seating inside the hotel are covered with sleeping bags

WORKING COLD

Each summer, the Ice Hotel melts away, only to be rebuilt again the following winter.

and animal skins, both for comfort and to help insulate the ice from the heat of the occupant's body. Cold drinks are served in glasses made of ice. Hot food, on the other hand, has to be served on more traditional plates.

ALTA IGLOO HOTEL

On a smaller scale, the Alta Igloo Hotel in Norway contains about twenty rooms. It is a full-service hotel with a chapel, gallery, bar, and other amenities. As with the Ice Hotel Jukkasjärvi, indoor temperatures of the igloo hover around 23 °F (–5 °C). Sleeping guests are made comfortable with thick animal skins and insulated sleeping bags.

Commercial ice hotels and igloos must maintain traditional buildings that house restrooms for obvious reasons. But this inconvenience does not deter visitors from seeking out this unique hotel experience.

ICE HOTEL QUEBEC

The sister hotel to Ice Hotel Jukkasjärvi is located near Quebec City in Canada. The annual construction cost for the Ice Hotel Quebec is in the neighborhood of $400,000, which is not much when compared to the price of building a permanent hotel. The Quebec hotel has a wedding chapel, a movie theater, and a ballroom, all constructed entirely of ice.

Ice Hotel Quebec undergoes a rapid construction season each year, usually lasting about five weeks. About 400 tons of ice and 12,000 tons of snow are required to build the structure and furnishings. The snow-packed structural walls vary in thickness up to about 6 feet (1.8 meters) deep. The main lobby boasts a high, vaulted ceiling, built to resemble an igloo dome. The resulting structure is simple, quite stable, and does not require elaborate interior supports. The hotel is roughly half the size of Ice Hotel Jukkasjärvi at about 30,000 square feet (3,000 square meters).

Ice has many uses, and architecture is perhaps one of the most interesting. Building entire structures out of seasonal materials is challenging enough without adding freezing temperatures into the mix. These hotels are increasingly popular and, while not for everyone, they have a small

The Ice Hotel and Snow Cathedral in Quebec, Canada, is a major wintertime tourist destination.

FREEZING POINT OF ALCOHOL

Both Ice Hotel Quebec and Ice Hotel Jukkasjärvi have vodka bars where vodka drinks are served in ice glasses. Why is vodka the alcoholic beverage of choice for an ice hotel? The freezing point of alcoholic liquids depends on the alcohol content. Pure ethanol freezes at about −200 °F (−128 °C). Vodka, which has an alcohol content of about 40 percent, freezes at −22 °F (−30 °C). Because of this high alcohol content, the freezing point of vodka is much lower than that of water, which freezes at 32 °F (0 °C). Vodka can therefore remain a liquid while being stored in the ice hotel.

Why not serve beer or sparkling wine? Beer averages about 6 percent alcohol by volume, so it would freeze at about 24 °F (−4 °C). However, even if the beer were stored at this temperature and did not freeze, it would freeze immediately upon opening the bottle. A bottle of carbonated beer has a certain temperature, volume, and pressure. To maintain a constant state, the relationship between pressure, temperature, and volume cannot change. This relationship is called the "ideal gas law," and is expressed in the formula $pV = nRT$, where p is pressure, V is volume, n is the amount of material, R is a constant, and T is the temperature.

Once a very cold, pressurized bottle is opened, the pressure inside the bottle decreases rapidly in an attempt to equalize the pressure on the outside of the bottle. As pressure goes down, so does temperature. If the liquid inside the bottle were already close to freezing, this fast drop in temperature would be enough to cause the liquid to freeze immediately. It is a fun phenomenon to watch, but perhaps not very much fun for patrons of the bar!

yet loyal following. Most accommodate only a small number of people at a time. Consider the difference from some of New York's largest skyscrapers, which can easily be occupied by thousands of people at one time. The World Trade Center towers, before their destruction in 2001, were home to nearly an acre of usable space on each of their more than 100 floors. They were architecture on a truly magnificent scale and, much like ice hotels, were emblematic of the culture that produced them.

ICE PALACE

One of the first large structures built entirely from ice was the Ice Palace commissioned by Russian Empress Anna Ivanova in the winter of 1739–1740, to celebrate the victory of Russia over Turkey. Georg Kraft, head of the St. Petersburg Academy of Sciences, assisted in the design and construction of the Ice Palace as a scientific experiment. The first attempt at building the Ice Palace on an ice-covered river failed when the roof caved in, causing the walls to collapse and flooding the site with water. The second, successful, version of the Ice Palace was built on the shore near the Winter Palace.

The Ice Palace was built on a large scale and was about 165 feet (50 meters) wide and 66 feet (20 meters) tall. It was built from large blocks of ice sawed from the Neva River. These blocks were stacked on top of each other and frozen together by pouring liquid water on them. The structure was then sculpted by stone carvers, who produced a realistic Baroque-styled façade on the Ice Palace, similar to buildings in the rest of St. Petersburg at the time. The building was reportedly extremely beautiful, with a marble-like appearance that changed to a translucent dark blue when struck by light. The interior was decorated with elaborate posts and statues, and divided into a number of large and small rooms. Windows were made from panes of clear ice.

The interior of the palace was filled with a variety of realistic furniture built completely from ice, including tables, chairs, and even beds and pillows. The furnishings were highly detailed, down to a deck of ice cards placed on an ice table. An ice fireplace with ice logs could actually burn, as the logs were smeared with oil; an ice bathtub was also functional. An outdoor garden was filled with ice trees and ice birds. In addition to its realistic furnishings, the Ice Palace had fantastic elements such as a life-sized ice elephant. During the day, the elephant served as a fountain, jetting water up to 12 feet (4 meters) in height. But at night, in contrast to the ice, the elephant gave off jets of burning oil. In addition to the elephant, the Ice Palace included icy dolphins with tongues of flame. Visitors to the palace were amazed by the contrast of fire and ice, which had been made possible by consultation with the scientist Kraft, who knew that oil could burn faster than ice could melt.

This painting shows the Empress Anna Ivanova, in the yellow dress at the center, dancing and entertaining in the Ice Palace at the wedding of her two court jesters (left).

The Ice Palace was reportedly used by Empress Anna Ivanova for entertaining during the festivities following the Russian defeat of Turkey. The structure survived until March 1740, when the warming weather caused the ice to begin to melt and the palace to droop. As expected, the melting began on the side of the palace facing the sun. The Empress Anna died later in 1740, but the Ice Palace lived on in a popular novel and later a film. A copy of the Ice Palace was built in 2000 for a Russian documentary production, using techniques similar to the original.

CHAPTER 5

REBUILDING A SYMBOL

The World Trade Center

The September 11, 2001, destruction of the World Trade Center in New York City is a well-known event. Many who did not experience it firsthand remember watching it live on television, and the images will remain with them forever. The story of the Twin Towers is a fascinating look at design innovation and engineering accomplishment.

ORIGINAL TWIN TOWERS

Before the destructive events of September 11, 2001, the Twin Towers of the World Trade Center dominated the Manhattan skyline.

The World Trade Center, including the two massive towers, was part of an urban renewal scheme in the 1950s. Brothers Nelson and David Rockefeller were the chief supporters of the project, insisting that it would help bring commerce and positive influences into lower Manhattan. Minoru Yamasaki was selected as the architect, and the plan for the complex was confirmed in 1962. Construction began in 1966.

The site was large by any standard, occupying more than sixteen acres. The original design included six buildings: the Twin Towers, the Vista Hotel, and three buildings that housed the U.S. Customs Service and other offices. Another office building was added in 1987. One of the more

MODERN WONDERS

The World Trade Center complex consisted of the two iconic towers—1 WTC and 2 WTC—as well as a number of smaller buildings.

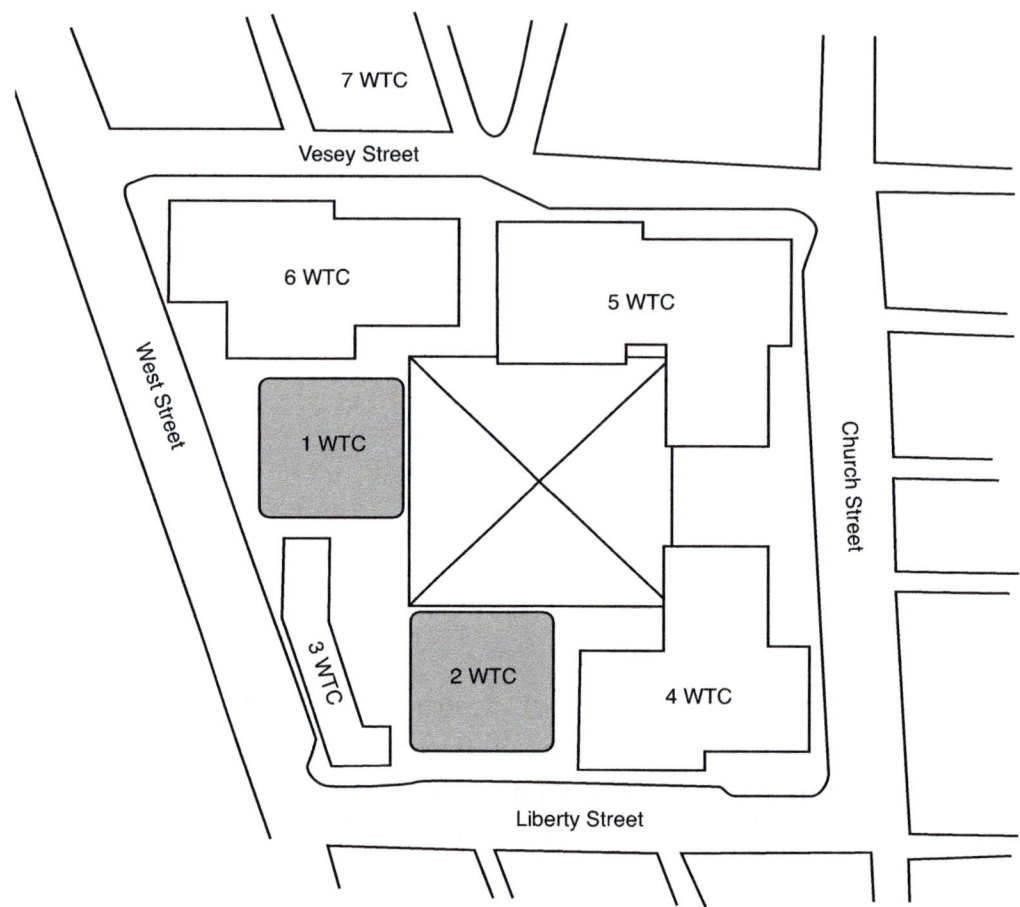

remarkable features of the site was an underground shopping mall and a hub for the subway and other transit systems.

The site became a center of activity in lower Manhattan. The amount of office space at the complex exceeded 13 million square feet (1.2 million square meters) where more than 50,000 people worked each day. The World Trade Center plaza was so enormous that it was eventually given its own zip code.

Excavation

A construction project of this scale requires a substantial amount of earth to be dug out and removed. Over 1.2 million cubic yards (900,000 cubic

REBUILDING A SYMBOL

The construction site for the World Trade Center complex in 1966.

meters) were excavated. Typically, when a large amount of earth is removed, it is used as landfill for new building sites. In this case the earth was relocated along the Hudson River, and much of Battery Park City was built on the resulting fill.

The excavation required several measures to ensure the safety of the people and other buildings in the vicinity, as well as the safety of the World Trade Center itself. Surrounding subway tunnels had to continue functioning during construction. There were also plans to store a large gold repository under the World Trade Center, so the six-level basement had to be breach-proof. The foundations were designed by the engineering department of the Port Authority of New York and New Jersey.

Structure and Construction

The World Trade Center's Twin Towers were designed to each contain 110 stories. The original plans called for slightly shorter buildings, but the race to create the tallest building in the world is ever alluring to building designers, and the plans were changed to add an additional 20 stories. One World Trade Center (the North Tower) had a 360-foot (110-meter) television antenna built into the top, which brought the total height to the then-world's tallest building to 1,368 feet (417 meters). While it immediately replaced the Empire State Building as the tallest skyscraper, the North Tower was soon outpaced by the Sears Tower in Chicago.

The structural design of the Twin Towers can be summed up as a steel tube. The chief structural engineer for the project was Leslie Robertson, a recognized New York engineer who was involved with the project from the mid-1960s. His network of columns and beams helped support the exterior structure and enveloped the interior core structure. Steel was the material of choice for the structural elements. Concrete is heavier, and

The World Trade Center was constructed with an interior structural core that provided stability and mechanical access. An outer series of structural columns supported the exterior facing and helped provide additional wind and shear resistance.

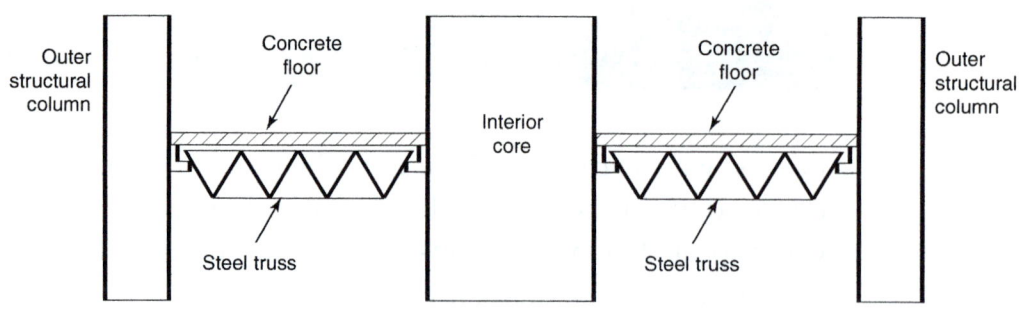

REBUILDING A SYMBOL

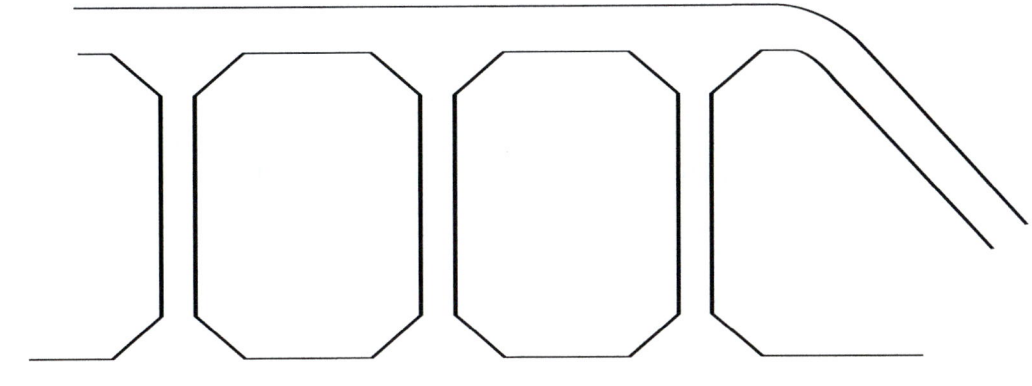

A type of truss called a Vierendeel truss, one with rigid instead of flexible joint connections, was used in the World Trade Center.

while it has excellent strength, using it to support all 110 floors would have made the buildings much too heavy.

In the design, steel columns (sixty-one placed along each side of each tower) and beams created a tube. The particular type of steel column used here is called a Vierendeel truss, and they were connected to each other using standard truss forms. Vierendeel trusses have been used in bridge design as well, and have stiff lower and upper beams with a

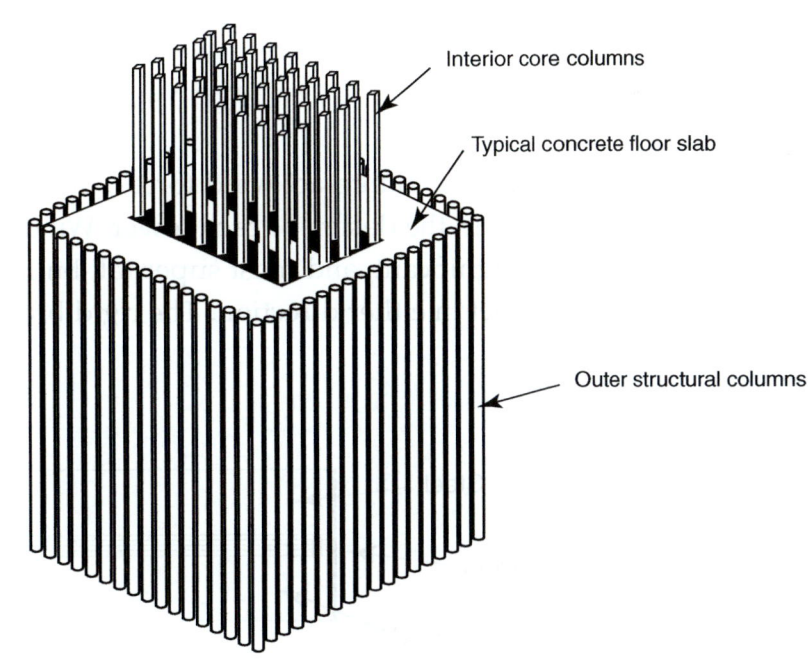

The interior core columns and outer structural columns shared the massive burden of supporting the structural and cladding elements of the World Trade Center.

67

vertical column connecting them. They differ from traditional trusses mainly in that they have no diagonal members. Their use in the World Trade Center is particularly interesting because it was one of the first large-scale uses of this building typology in a tall vertical structure. The main structural goal of the Vierendeel trusses was to absorb horizontal shear force (in this case, supplied mainly by the wind) and to help create a rigid overall structure. The trussed columns were fabricated in approximately two-story segments off-site and then transported to the site and installed.

Each individual exterior column of the Twin Towers was designed to support its own weight, and together they supported half the weight of the levels above them. The interior core was made up of more columns and beams. These columns supported themselves and the other half of the floor weight, as well as the interior building systems. This lightweight structure allowed the exterior wind bracing to function most efficiently; it was capable of withstanding wind loads without having to transfer them into the core, which was doing most of the building support work.

The steel frames were clad using a glass system. Floor slabs were made of concrete positioned on more steel trusses. Each tower used about 100,000 tons of steel.

COUNTERING THE WIND FORCE

In order to further counteract wind forces, more than 10,000 dampers were included in the design of each tower. Wind forces that act on skyscrapers are significant, and most super-tall buildings are designed to move a few feet in either direction. The rigid bracing of the Vierendeel

Dampers were attached to the lower chord of the World Trade Center tower trusses. They consisted of steel plates sandwiching a viscoelastic layer, and absorbed the lateral motion of the building.

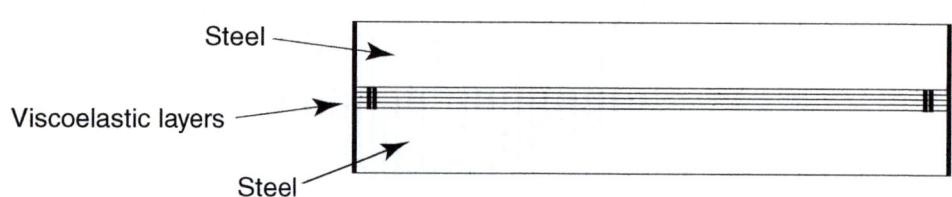

trusses helped resist wind forces because they allowed the entire structure to move as a cohesive unit rather than shifting in pieces, like a chain. But even further efforts were required in order to keep the building's tenants from feeling the building sway.

Each of the trusses of the exterior columns in the Twin Towers had a damper on the lower chord (the chord is the lower horizontal component of the truss). Each damper is made of steel plates that enclose a viscoelastic layer, which consists of shock-absorbing material. Elastic materials deform when they are squeezed or stretched, but return quickly to their original configuration. Viscoelastic materials can also be deformed, but they absorb extra energy that is dissipated in the form of frictional heating. Viscoelastic materials can therefore absorb, or dampen, excess energy.

In the case of a tall building, the viscoelastic material acts to absorb the motion of the building elements, reducing the total distance that the building would otherwise move in reaction to wind forces. When the wind pushes against a building, the upper and lower truss chords are able to rotate independently, thus keeping the sway of the entire building to a minimum.

1975 FIRE

One of the first major incidents to affect the Twin Towers was a February 13, 1975, fire in the North Tower. It started on the eleventh floor around midnight, apparently set by an irate custodian, and burned for three hours, affecting parts of six other floors. Fifty people were evacuated, but there were no fatalities. Sprinkler systems and other methods of fire suppression were installed shortly afterward, as they were not part of the initial design. Building codes for skyscraper fire safety are constantly evolving, and they tend to get stricter in the aftermath of a disaster such as this one.

Settlement

A major concern with any super-tall structure is settlement, or the way the building sinks into the foundation soil over time. All buildings settle to some degree, as they reach their full height and full occupancy loads. The goal is for a building to settle evenly, at roughly the same rate (and to the same depth) over its entire base. Uneven settling could occur if the original excavations resulted in uneven terrain or if the building loads are designed very asymmetrically.

In the case of the Twin Towers, settlement was a major concern because much of lower Manhattan is built on landfill. Given the enormous weight of the towers (some estimates put each building's load at 500,000 tons), the foundations had to be dug down more than 70 feet (21 meters), well into bedrock, to minimize the risk of uneven settlement. Since bedrock consists of a single strong rigid element, rather than the varying elements found in fill, it provides a much safer and sturdier support for a foundation.

1993 BOMBING

The first terrorist attack on the World Trade Center occurred on February 26, 1993. Ramzi Yousef of Pakistan was convicted in 1998 of bombing the North Tower. An explosives-filled truck was parked in the underground garage and then detonated, killing six people and injuring many more. Four of the concrete sublevels were damaged when a hole nearly 100 feet wide was blown open. Smoke rose to the ninety-third floor of both towers, and there was damage to electrical and telephone lines, although the damage was minimal. A memorial to those lost was later built in the form of a granite reflecting pool.

September 11, 2001, Terrorist Attacks

On the morning of September 11, 2001, hijackers flew Boeing commercial airliners into each of the Twin Towers. The towers withstood the initial impact, but the North Tower, which was hit at 8:45 A.M., collapsed at 10:28 A.M. The South Tower was hit at 9:03 A.M. and collapsed at 9:59 A.M. The attacks directly caused 2,749 fatalities with the potential for more future deaths due to inhalation of smoke and particles at the site.

Immediately after impact, fires began to rage within the towers. Whether due to jet-fuel ignition or the ignition of the aluminum from the aircraft bodies, the fires were extremely hot. Steel softens at 797 °F (425 °C) and loses some of its strength by 1,200 °F (650 °C). The melting point of steel is about 2,750 °F (1,510 °C). Once the fire exceeded about 1,200 °F in parts of the towers, the steel distorted and began to buckle. As the steel frame gave way, the towers lost their support, and the floors located around the impact sites began to collapse.

Each floor in the towers weighed about 4,500 tons and was designed to support its own weight plus about 1,300 tons. Once several floors collapsed and fell onto the floors beneath them, their combined weight soon became more than any single floor could support, so the towers collapsed.

The towers were designed to withstand lateral wind loads of about 5,000 tons. They were "redundant" structures, which means that there was more structure than was needed to simply support the building. If a few interior or exterior columns became damaged, the rest of the building would be able to make up for it by redistributing the loads. The World Trade Center towers were also designed to withstand the impact of an airliner. However, the plans for the structural systems for the towers were created in 1966, and at that time the largest commercial airliner was a Boeing 707.

Despite all the safety features incorporated in the design of the World Trade Center towers, they were simply unable to withstand the double blow of the events of September 11. The structure of the towers was weakened by the airplane impacts, and they were ultimately destroyed

MODERN WONDERS

The structure of the towers held up to the initial airplane impacts of September 11, and allowed thousands of people to escape. However, the towers were no match for the high-intensity fires produced by jet fuel from the planes, and they eventually fell.

by the long-lived, extremely hot-burning fires fueled by the large amounts of jet fuel in the tanks of the huge, long-range airplanes that struck shortly after they took off from Boston. No one could have foreseen an attack of this magnitude when the towers were planned. It is a testament to their design that they stood long enough after the impact to allow the majority of their occupants to escape.

HOW THE TOWERS FELL

At the time of the attacks, news reports often mentioned how "lucky" it was that the World Trade Center towers did not fall sideways onto other buildings in the surrounding areas. There is a scientific explanation for why they could not have fallen sideways. Consider first that much of the space occupied by the building, close to 95 percent, was air; the space taken up by the structure itself was minimal compared to the volume of the building. This is important to understand because a solid block of steel would have reacted very differently to the airplane strike, since it would have had a different mass and density.

Any tall building contains a considerable amount of gravitational potential energy because of the amount of heavy material located high off the ground. Potential energy is stored energy; gravitational potential energy is the potential energy resulting from an object's vertical height above the surface of the earth. It is related to mass by the equation

$$PE_{grav} = m \times g \times h$$

where m = mass of the object, g = acceleration due to gravity (9.8 m/s^2 on earth), and h = height of the object.

The gravitational force is a direct correlation between the weight of the object and the earth's gravitational pull:

$$F_{grav} = m \times g$$

where m = mass of the object and g = acceleration due to gravity (9.8 m/s^2 on earth).

The strength of the Twin Towers' steel frames ordinarily kept them from falling over under nonstress conditions, or regular daily life for a skyscraper. After the attacks, when fire caused the steel to buckle, the potential energy of the undamaged skyscraper was converted into kinetic energy when the top floors started moving downward under the force of gravity. The upper floors gained momentum, a value that is determined by a combination of the weight of an object and how fast it is traveling. Momentum is calculated as

$$P = m \times v$$

where m = mass of the object and v = velocity of the object.

Once the floors began falling and converted their potential energy into kinetic energy, their energy was that of an object in motion, defined as

$$KE = \tfrac{1}{2} \times m \times v^2$$

where m = mass of the object and v = velocity of the object.

As the materials from the upper floors fell, they picked up speed due to the increased mass of the combined floors, as well as the acceleration due to gravity. When they hit the remaining nonbuckling floors, the force of this impact coupled with the weight of the material from the upper floors was more than the lower floors could support, and successive floors kept falling. Since gravity was the only force acting on the materials at this point, they fell straight down and not sideways.

REBUILDING

Efforts to redesign and replace the World Trade Center began as the enormous task of cleaning up the site was still under way. The Lower Manhattan Development Corporation worked to sponsor an international design competition. The design for a single new Freedom Tower by architect Daniel Libeskind was accepted. The rest of the plaza also will be rebuilt, with different architects designing various parts of it.

One of the most remarkable aspects of the Twin Towers was their sheer size. Tall and thin, sleek and elegant, the towers rose toward the sky and became the quintessential symbols of New York. Elsewhere in the country, other monuments take on that same role, though they manifest their greatness in very different ways. Mount Rushmore is one of the most famous tributes to America, yet it bears no resemblance to New York's skyscrapers. Like Mount Rushmore, however, the Twin Towers will always remain an unforgettable symbol of their time.

The Pentagon

One of the country's most impressive government buildings, the Pentagon (located in Arlington, Virginia) was designed as a five-sided fortress for the War Department, today better known as the Department of Defense. Events occurring abroad in the first half of the twentieth century, including Hitler's rise to power, spurred the creation of an increasingly large American military workforce; this massive building strove to meet those demands.

The building was completed in 1943 and involved a construction effort that required more than 13,000 workers. Today it is one of the largest office buildings in the world—more than 26,000 people, both civilians and military, have offices in the Pentagon, and the parking lot can accommodate more than 8,000 vehicles. The Pentagon occupies nearly thirty acres, and has resulted in many local building projects, including highways and bridges. The building is like its own city, complete with shopping and restaurants.

The key to understanding the conceptual layout of the Pentagon is the number five. The building has five sides to accommodate the five major roads leading to the building. The interior design is based on five concentric rings, which are labeled alphabetically from the inside out; the innermost ring is the A-ring, while the outermost is the E-ring. There are F- and G-ring additions, located at the basement level. Navigating the Pentagon requires practice. The offices are numbered clock-

The Pentagon's structure was damaged due to the airplane impact on September 11, 2001, but its design allowed the damage to be confined primarily to one wedge.

wise for each ring, and the offices are also annotated by their proximity to a corridor.

The terrorist attacks of September 11, 2001, had severe consequences not only for the World Trade Center, but also for the Pentagon. American Airlines Flight 77 was hijacked and subsequently flown into the western façade of the Pentagon. A large fire broke out, and one portion of the building collapsed. Fortunately, that part of the building was undergoing renovation at the time, so it was largely unoccupied, but more than 100 people from the Pentagon lost their lives, in addition to the passengers and crew on the plane.

The Pentagon was designed to be extremely resistant to attacks, and the fact that a Boeing 757 full of fuel could crash into the building without more damage shows the strength of that design. For example, the exterior walls of the Pentagon are 24 inches (61 cm) thick, including 6 inches (15 cm) of Indiana limestone on the outside, followed by 8 inches (20 cm) of brick, and then 10 inches (25 cm) of concrete. The floors of the Pentagon are 5.5 inches (14 cm) thick and are supported by concrete columns spaced every 20 feet (6 meters).

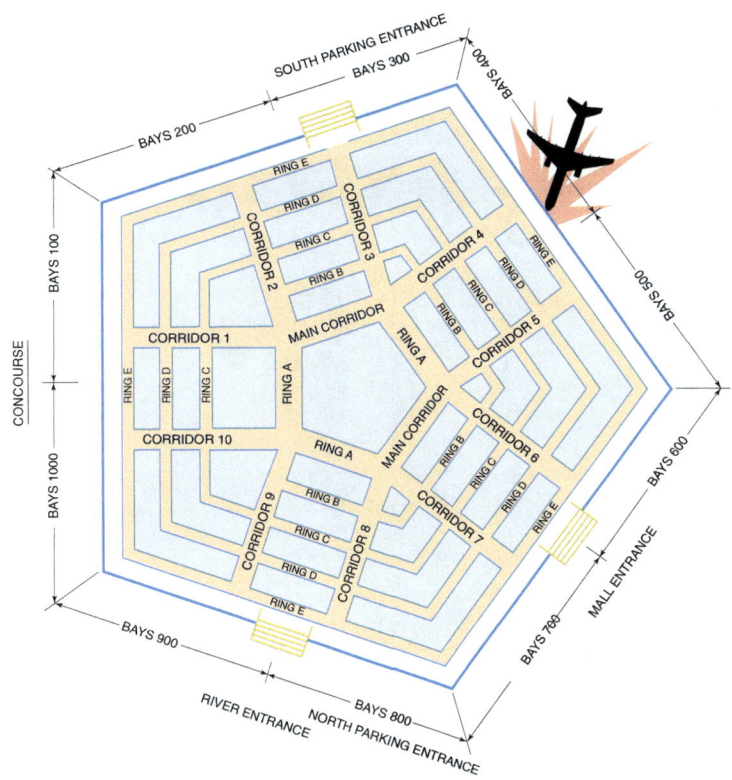

The Pentagon's design includes five concentric rings, along with radial structures that divide the building into wedges.

Since the Pentagon Renovation Project was ongoing at the time of the attack, the project was expanded to include the necessary repairs from the airplane damage. The areas destroyed by the crash were torn down and rebuilt; these repairs took about a year, after which time the Pentagon occupants were able to return to their offices.

CHAPTER 6

STONE GIANTS

Mount Rushmore National Memorial

Abraham Lincoln's nose, part of the Mount Rushmore National Memorial in South Dakota, is cleaned every other year along with the rest of the monument.

Throughout history, civilizations have left behind architectural masterpieces—from the ancient Mesoamerican pyramids to modern skyscrapers. Stonehenge in England was the epitome of simplicity, elegance, science, and nature; the same could be said about the Parthenon in Athens, though these two monuments are entirely different.

Art also gives insight into a civilization. From cave paintings to stained glass to more traditional sculpture and portraiture, artists have used whatever technology and materials were at their disposal to create lasting representations of their achievements. Many works of art are emblematic of the period in which they were created.

The Mount Rushmore National Memorial in the Black Hills of South Dakota bridges the gap between the architectural and artistic worlds. This massive stone carving represents the nation's achievements as well as those of the people who created the monument. It commemorates some of the most important presidents in the history of the United States and is often seen as a tribute to democracy. It is also a masterful display of stone carving on a very large scale.

ORIGIN OF THE IDEA

The concept for Mount Rushmore originated with Doane Robinson (1856–1946), a Minnesota farmer and South Dakota state historian who later became a lawyer. Seeing that the Black Hills were already an attraction, Robinson thought carving a mammoth sculpture into the side of the mountain would increase the popularity of the region.

Robinson's first thought as to the design of the site actually had nothing to do with the presidents. He proposed carving statues of several early pioneers, but Gutzon Borglum, the sculptor Robinson commissioned for the project, overturned this idea. A talented artist with a strong personality, Borglum thought it would make more sense to sculpt something of truly national interest, and hence was born the idea to carve portraits of four of the nation's presidents. George Washington, Thomas Jefferson, Theodore Roosevelt, and Abraham Lincoln were chosen to represent, respectively, the nation's independence, democratic process, leadership in world affairs, and equality.

Initially, Robinson had thought to construct the monument at a site that featured large granite pillars, called needles. His vision was to have each of these carved into an individual statue. Borglum insisted that the monument would be more powerful if it were carved out of a single mountain. The current site was confirmed and work commenced around 1927, after a formal dedication by President Calvin Coolidge. Financing was a major problem until 1929, when President Coolidge enacted legislation to create a formal committee that would lead the fundraising and construction efforts.

The site of the Black Hills originally belonged to Native Americans. The Lakota, one of the Sioux tribes, occupied many parts of the Dakotas and Minnesota. The mountain chosen for the monument was known as Six Grandfathers and was an important religious site for the Lakota. It was taken by the U.S. government in 1876 following a series of military campaigns. The rightful ownership of the site remains a point of contention today for the Lakota Sioux. In 1885, American businessman Charles Rushmore visited the area, and the mountain was given his name. Rushmore later donated a sizable sum to the monument project.

STONE GIANTS

Sculptor Gutzon Borglum, shown here at the White House in 1924, designed the monuments at Mount Rushmore.

Sculptor Gutzon Borglum (1867–1941) was Robinson's ultimate choice for the project. Raised in the state of Nebraska, Borglum was the son of Danish immigrants. He studied art in San Francisco and Paris, and his bronze sculpture *The Mares of Diomedes* was the first piece of American sculpture purchased by the Metropolitan Museum of Art in New York.

Geology

The geological conditions at the Mount Rushmore site presented many challenges for the workers. The bedrock consisted of two primary layers: an upper granite layer and a bottom mica schist layer. Granite is an igneous rock (a rock created from heat, usually from a melted material) consisting of the minerals quartz, feldspar, and mica. It often has a visibly crystalline appearance. Mica is the name for a collection of minerals that, when cut, split easily into thin sheets. Mica schist is a variant of mica that also includes quartz and feldspar.

The granite at the Mount Rushmore site is quite old, dating back at least 2 billion years. The Black Hills were originally formed of sand and clay. Early in geological time, most of the land that would become the United States was underwater, and as the seas receded around the continent of North America, erosion acted quickly to eat away at this sandy material. Some material was buried as more eroded grains were deposited on top, and over time it was gradually compressed into sandstone.

A plume of melted material from the center of the earth gradually rose to the surface around one and a half billion years ago, and granite was formed. This is what created the base for Mount Rushmore. The quartz and other materials found today at the site were created by the contact between this melted rock and the existing compressed sandstone. The rocks changed structure as a result of the added pressure of this new material, allowing the formation of mica, feldspar, and other minerals.

The landscape of the Black Hills is the result of erosion. Over the last billion years, wind, snow, ice, and rain have gradually taken away bits of the rocks. Another reason for the jagged appearance of the hills is that some new rocks were gradually deposited at the site, probably as the sea receded from the area. As water levels continued to fall, sediment and dissolved compounds precipitating from the evaporating ocean created new mineral formations.

Will Mount Rushmore completely erode away during our lifetime? Probably not, since erosion is a very slow process. It is estimated that about one inch of rock is removed from the Black Hills every 8,000 to 10,000 years. This is one of the reasons that the Black Hills were such a good site for the Mount Rushmore monument. Compared to other minerals, granite is very hard and resistant to erosion, and it made an excellent base for the massive sculpture.

Construction

As part of their working-design methodology, architects typically build a scale model of a structure before actually proceeding to the construction phase of a project. This model helps designers evaluate their work, and also helps the patrons to "see" a project before its design is confirmed. Borglum built a plaster scale model that allowed workers to get a sense of the overall picture before proceeding to the details that they would chisel from the stone.

STONE GIANTS

Borglum's original scale model of Mount Rushmore included waist-high busts of the four presidents.

One of the first construction challenges the project faced was how to get workers up the side of the mountain. When carving sculptures more than 60 feet (18 meters) tall, it was necessary to design a way for all 400 workers to easily get up and down the mountain. Stairs and ramps were used initially, and a tram was later constructed for moving supplies and equipment (and ultimately workers) to the top of the mountain.

Gutzon Borglum was the master artist for the project, but he did not do the actual carving. He was responsible for translating his designs, on paper and in models, onto the massive surface of the rocks and for supervising the work. Borglum was often seen scaling nearby mountains to determine the details for the sculpture as they would have been seen from a distance.

Most of the construction took place during the Great Depression, and the majority of the carvers were former or out-of-work miners. The carvers had to work long hours, starting early in the morning to take advantage of the daylight. Since the sculpture of Mount Rushmore faced

MODERN WONDERS

Borglum (hanging below the eye) and his crew at work in the 1930s carving the head of Abraham Lincoln.

southeast, they were presented with many hours of sunlight. They were allowed to start working slightly later in the day during the fall and winter months because the sun had to be high enough in the sky to provide sufficient illumination.

HALL OF RECORDS

Early monuments and buildings were built for eternity—structures like the Egyptian and Mayan pyramids have lasted for thousands of years and will likely endure many thousands more before they erode back into sand. Most buildings from the twentieth century, however, will not endure like those ancient structures. Modern houses and skyscrapers are built from materials like steel and reinforced concrete that will corrode and crumble if left unattended for tens or hundreds, rather than thousands, of years. Mount Rushmore was designed to be an enduring monument, and Borglum thought it would be a good location for a Hall of Records that would safeguard some national treasures such as the Declaration of Independence. He began excavation on what was supposed to be a large chamber behind and below the famous faces, but ran out of time and money and never finished the project. In 1998, the Borglum family and the National Park Service finally finished construction on a scaled-down Hall of Records that contains a vault made of titanium. Inside the vault are tablets made from porcelain that contain the words of the Declaration of Independence, the Constitution, and a history of the United States, among others. This vault, and Mount Rushmore itself, could be an enduring message to a future civilization.

Creating the Work

The rocks of Mount Rushmore had to be prepared before carving could begin. Huge amounts of rock were removed and the remainder smoothed out. It would not have been practical for workers to manually remove such large pieces of rock, so dynamite was used to blast away the largest chunks.

MODERN WONDERS

The 1929 construction on Mount Rushmore began with controlled blasting of unnecessary rock.

Once the face of the stone was close to the required size, the workers started drilling. Pieces of rock were drilled with jackhammers rather than chiseled away. Chiseling would have required more manual effort, while the jackhammers were less precise and had to be handled with care. As soon as the drilling process finished, chiselers came onto the job. These were the more skilled workers who did the final phases of the project that would ultimately reveal the faces of the presidents. They used smaller drilling tools to complete a process called honeycombing. A series of holes was drilled into the rock in a grid, and the pieces of rock in between the holes were then removed. Once the honeycombing was completed, pneumatic hammers were used to shape the sculpture details.

To position themselves properly for the carving, workers took a top-down approach. After arriving at the top of the mountain, they were

STONE GIANTS

strapped into harnesses and then winched themselves down to the appropriate spot on the mountain's face. An operator at the top of the mountain guided this winching process. While safety was more or less ensured, and no lives were lost in the entire construction process, it was sometimes difficult for the workers to stay aligned with the operator above.

How did workers know exactly which faces to carve, and to what depth? This task was made easier by Borglum's model and system of measurements. To aid in the translation of his design into reality, Borglum superimposed a grid of small boxes onto his model. The grid had coordinates along the horizontal (x) and vertical (y) axes, like a plot on a piece of graph paper. On this grid, Borglum marked a location along the x and y axis for each point to be carved. He also marked the angle at which the element should be carved. These measurements were then scaled up to the much larger size of the actual mountain, and gave workers the location for each box of the grid. These coordinates enabled the

Today the heads of George Washington, Thomas Jefferson, Theodore Roosevelt, and Abraham Lincoln are clearly visible at Mount Rushmore.

workers to make accurate carvings at every point along the face of the mountain.

While Borglum was the master of this design, he unfortunately did not live to see his creation fully realized. He died before construction was completed, but his son, Lincoln, saw the job through to its eventual completion in October 1941.

THE FAMOUS FACES

Who were the presidents that Borglum and Robinson decided to immortalize on the face of Mount Rushmore? George Washington, Thomas Jefferson, Abraham Lincoln, and Theodore Roosevelt were chosen for their contributions to America, their outstanding achievements, and their central position in the creation of democracy in the United States.

George Washington was the first president of the United States and served between 1789 and 1797. He was born to a family of Virginia planters and by 1754 was a lieutenant colonel in the military. He became commander-in-chief of the army in 1775 and worked tirelessly to assert American independence from the British. He was also the main proponent of America's neutrality in the war between France and England that took place as part of the French Revolution.

Thomas Jefferson, the third U.S. president, was secretary of state under George Washington and served as president between 1801 and 1809. Jefferson was also the son of Virginia planters and later entered political and military life. He sided with the French during the French Revolution, and played a major role in the development of the first two political parties in the United States: the Democratic-Republicans and the Federalists. The latter supported France in the war and was in favor of individual states' rights.

Abraham Lincoln was the sixteenth president, serving between 1861 and 1865. He presided over the country during the Civil War, when southern Confederate states attempted to secede from the Union. By 1860 he won the presidency on the Republican ticket, and in 1863 he issued the Emancipation Proclamation. This freed the slaves in the southern Confederate states.

STONE GIANTS

Left to right: George Washington, president of the United States between 1789 and 1797; Thomas Jefferson, president of the United States between 1801 and 1809; Abraham Lincoln, president of the United States between 1861 and 1865; Theodore Roosevelt, president of the United States between 1901 and 1909.

Theodore Roosevelt, the twenty-sixth president of the United States, served between 1901 and 1909. He was a leader in world affairs and also increased the role the government played in keeping the peace between employers and employees. Roosevelt made possible the building of the Panama Canal, mediated the Russo-Japanese War, and also did more than any president before him to conserve national lands.

The details of carving a sculpture on the scale of Mount Rushmore are scarcely comprehensible. Because it was carved over such a long period of time, its progress likely appeared very slow and somewhat mysterious to the casual observer, but eventually the final form of the sculpture would be evident. This gradual unveiling of such a work, while typical of sculpture, is very different from the construction of a mechanical object such as a Ferris wheel. While also monumental in nature and equally impressive in terms of human accomplishment and design, Ferris wheels are mechanical expressions of their very natures. Mount Rushmore, in a way, hides all the work that went into it, but a masterpiece such as the Millennium Wheel (see Chapter 7) shows every detail of its construction.

CHAPTER 7

ROUND THEY GO

The Millennium Wheel

The Millennium Wheel, also known as the London Eye, is an observation wheel in London that opened to the public in 2000.

A highlight of summer for children around the world is a trip to the amusement park. The delights at a theme park are plentiful: merry-go-rounds, roller coasters, spinning teacups, and water dips. While not for the faint of heart (or faint of stomach), amusement park rides are designed to toss and turn the riders as much as possible within safety limitations.

The Ferris wheel is an amusement park standard that comes without the racing heart and lost pocket change. A Ferris wheel is a large rotating wheel with seating compartments. These compartments are at least partially enclosed and are spaced evenly around the wheel's circumference. In a typical Ferris wheel, passengers enter the compartment that is at the bottom. The wheel then rotates, allowing the next car's passengers to disembark and new passengers to enter the car. This process continues until the cars are filled with new riders; then the wheel will travel uninterrupted for a time so the passengers can enjoy their ride.

EARLY HISTORY

The world's first Ferris wheels existed long before the time of George Washington Ferris, the inventor of the amusement park ride. It is thought that as early as about 400 B.C.E., water wheels used for crop irrigation were commandeered by children looking for a ride. Writings from this period suggest that large wheels were also used in the production of grains and for distributing water to cities for use in operating sawmills and other early factories.

The original Ferris wheel was built in 1893 for the World Exposition in Chicago. It was designed by George Ferris.

One of the first documented appearances of a wheel designed for amusement was noted in 1620 by Englishman Peter Mundy. On a trip to Turkey, he wrote of a rotating wheel with people swinging from precarious seats. It would have been far from meeting today's safety standards, but it likely planted the idea in someone's mind to create such a device on a large scale.

About 200 years after Mr. Mundy's observations, wheels began to appear in the United States. The size of the wheels increased, and limited numbers were produced. None, however, became a stand-out model for manufacturers to follow. All this changed in 1893, with the World's Columbian Exposition in Chicago. This fair commemorated the 400th anniversary of Christopher Columbus's expedition to the New World, and it was a momentous occasion for all of American culture. Among the many other inventions to be displayed at this exposition was the world's biggest and best wheel.

The ride was designed by George Washington Ferris, a steel bridge builder who was in Chicago when the goals of the World Exposition were announced. He proposed his design for a gargantuan wheel that would take passengers on a circular ride that, among other things, promised excellent views from the top. Once his design was approved, Ferris immediately began selecting steelworkers to start making the Ferris wheel a reality.

Ferris Wheel Construction

Initial construction posed some difficulty. Because they were building in the middle of winter, the ground was either wet or frozen to a depth of more than 20 feet (6 meters). After pumping water out of the site, Ferris sank piles deep into the soil and then constructed massive foundations of reinforced concrete.

The major support for the Ferris wheel was provided by 140-foot (43-meter) towers that supported the axle; the wheel had to be completely suspended above the ground or it could not turn. The steel axle measured 45 feet (14 meters) long, with a diameter of nearly 3 feet (1 meter). It was the largest single piece of forged steel in existence at the time.

MODERN WONDERS

The wheel was constructed as a giant 250-foot (76-meter) steel ring. The cars attached to the wheel were also large by modern standards, measuring 24 x 13 x 10 feet (7 x 4 x 3 meters) high. Large windows allowed the passengers to enjoy sweeping views. In contrast to modern cars, a conductor rode in each compartment along with the passengers. Each revolution took about twenty minutes.

The original Ferris wheel was steam-driven by two engines; the steam for the engines was produced off-site and fed to the engines through

THE STEAM ENGINE

How is energy created in a steam engine? First, consider the differences between types of energy. Potential energy is stored energy: When a brick is held overhead, before it is dropped the brick stores potential energy. This particular kind of potential energy is called gravitational potential energy, or positional potential energy, because it comes from the position of the object. When the brick is dropped, that potential energy is converted into kinetic energy, or the energy that comes from objects in motion. Work is any force that causes an object to change position. If the brick is placed on a table and pushed from behind, you are doing work by causing the brick to move. Steam engines take potential energy in the form of water heated to the point of producing steam and use the components of the engine to convert this energy into work.

Diagrammatically, steam engines are simple to understand. In a typical steam engine, water is boiled to create steam. As the steam expands, a piston is pushed up. As the steam contracts, the piston falls. This rising and falling of the piston can do many different types of work, including the turning of a wheel. One of the disadvantages of the steam engine was the time required to pressurize the steam; this problem was overcome with later designs for a gasoline-powered engine.

pipes. The steam engine was the most efficient means to power the wheel at the time. The basic idea behind a steam engine is to convert potential energy into mechanical work—in this case, the force that would cause the wheel to turn.

After the exposition closed, the original Ferris wheel was sold and moved to another location, but it was destroyed about ten years later due to lack of interest and use.

WHEEL LAYOUT

How many seats does a typical Ferris wheel hold? The answer depends on the number of passenger cars and the size of the wheel. The circumference of the wheel can be calculated as the irrational number pi (π) times the diameter of the circle (*d*). Since the diameter is simply twice the radius of the circle, the circumference *C* can also be calculated as pi times twice the radius of the circle (*r*):

$$C = \pi d \quad or \quad C = 2\pi r$$

It is also important to remember that when the passenger cars are hanging in their vertical position, they cannot be able to touch each another. Spaced equally and safely, thirty-six cars could fit on a 250-foot (76-meter) wheel such as the 1893 Columbian Exposition wheel. With a maximum of forty people per car, the entire wheel could hold 1,440 people at a time.

FERRIS WHEEL PHYSICS

The passenger cars on a Ferris wheel must be specially designed to move around a pivot as the wheel rotates. If the cars were fixed, passengers would find themselves upside down at the top of the wheel! Instead, as the wheel rotates, the cars slowly reorient under the force of gravity so that they are always correctly positioned. In some cases, if the wheel rotates quickly enough, there is a lag between the wheel's motion and the

MODERN WONDERS

Cars on a Ferris wheel must pivot so that the riders remain right side up. At the top of the wheel, the bottom of the car points toward the center of the wheel, while at the bottom of the wheel the top of the car points toward the center of the wheel.

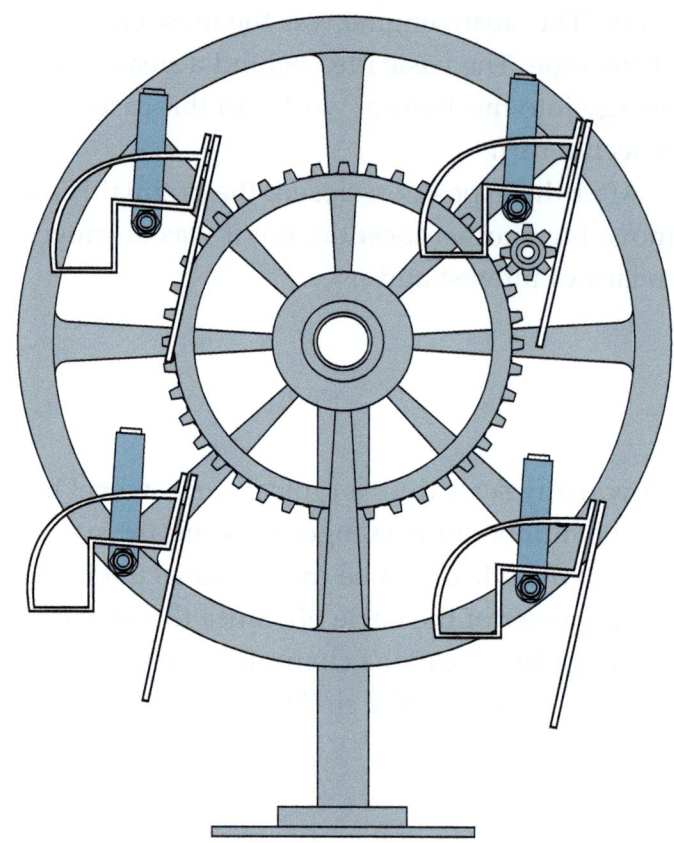

car's rotation due to friction at the rotation point and the inertia of the cars. In this case, the cars tend to tilt outward as the wheel rotates, giving the passengers a bit of a fun ride.

Another physical principle that can be illustrated with a Ferris wheel is centripetal motion. When an object is moving in a circle, it experiences acceleration toward the center of the circle called centripetal acceleration. Because this acceleration always points toward the center of the circle and gravity always points down, these two components act in different ways at different points on the circle. Centripetal force (F_c) is defined as

$$F_c = mv^2/r$$

where m is the mass of the person on the Ferris wheel, v is the velocity of the wheel, and r is the radius of the wheel.

In addition to their magnitude, forces also have a direction associated with them. When adding forces, it is important to take their directions into account as well as their sizes. In the case of centripetal motion, acceleration and gravity can point in different directions. At the top of the wheel, the centripetal force is subtracted from the F_g, or gravitational force ($F_g = ma$, where m is the mass and a is the acceleration). Since one force points up and the other points down at this location, one force is given a negative sign before they are combined. This means that the net force on a person at the top of the Ferris wheel is reduced, so a person riding a Ferris wheel while sitting on a bathroom scale would find that her weight was reduced at the top of the wheel. At the bottom of the wheel, the gravitational force and the centripetal force are added together, since they both point in the same direction there, and the person's weight would be increased.

PORTABLE WHEELS

Most county-fair–caliber Ferris wheels are designed for ease of transport rather than longevity. These wheels are typically much smaller than the original 1893 Exposition wheel. Most have a wheel diameter of about 60 feet (18 meters) and carry about fifty passengers when fully loaded. Portable Ferris wheels must be transported in a truck, assembled on-site, then disassembled and moved to the next location. Flexibility and fast construction are major requirements.

A portable Ferris wheel contains all the standard elements. Since permanent piles and foundations cannot be constructed, the base is usually anchored into a wheeled trailer. Steel towers are then assembled and attached to the trailer. Tension spokes are constructed; these lead from the central axle area to the outer rim of the wheel, where they will later be connected to seats. Inner and outer steel rings complete the visual structure of the Ferris wheel, though tensioning posts or other devices may also be used. Axles, brakes, electrical wiring, and other safety equipment are put into place as appropriate during the construction process.

Triple Wheel

A variation on the standard Ferris wheel is an invention from the 1970s called the triple Ferris wheel. First developed by the Swedish design company Intamin AG, this type of wheel was used at amusement parks in the United States as well. The ride was known as the Sky Whirl and consisted of three large mechanical arms, each of which was attached to a wheel that held a number of suspended passenger compartments. The arms extended out like branches from a large tower. The main advantage of this ride over a traditional Ferris wheel was that the wheels could be lowered to the ground on their sides and all passengers in a given wheel could be loaded and unloaded at once, rather than requiring the entire wheel to stop and unload each compartment one at a time. This ride is no longer in use today; it has been replaced by newer and faster rides.

The Millennium Wheel

The world's largest Ferris wheel is the British Airways Millennium Wheel. Built in 1999 to commemorate the beginning of the twenty-first century, it is also called the London Eye. This mammoth wheel reaches a whopping height of 443 feet (135 meters) and is positioned on the bank of the Thames River. Its location and size mean that spectacular views are available from many points along the ride.

The Millennium Wheel was created by a team of designers and was originally intended as a five-year display. It attracted so many visitors that its permit was extended indefinitely. It is not a speedy amusement park ride by any stretch of the imagination; it takes about thirty minutes to complete one revolution. There are thirty-two passenger cars around the circumference of the wheel, and each one is air-conditioned for rider comfort. The wheel can hold 800 passengers when fully loaded.

Most Ferris wheels have planned stops so that riders can board and disembark. The Millennium Wheel rotates so slowly, however, that it typically does not stop. Riders are able to hop on and off easily as the wheel continues to turn. The wheel does have brakes and can be stopped for emergencies or for people with disabilities.

ROUND THEY GO

The Millennium Wheel is the world's largest Ferris wheel and is located on the banks of the Thames River in London. When fully loaded, the Millennium Wheel can hold 800 passengers.

Structure of the Millennium Wheel

The structure of the Millennium Wheel is similar to that of a bicycle wheel. A stiff outer metal rim uses tie rods as its primary means of structural support; these bars carry a tension force that helps keep the rim in a stable position. Tie rods are always in tension, meaning they are always pushing against the axle and rim. Were they to absorb compression forces as well, they would be crushed, and the wheel would be prone to collapse.

The passenger capsules are connected to pipes that span the distance between the two large parallel wheels that comprise the frame system. The capsules are attached to circular mounting rings that are in turn attached to the outside of the main ring. This attachment system means

99

MODERN WONDERS

A rider on a Ferris wheel feels a different force at the top and the bottom of the ride. Since the force of gravity always points down, but the force exerted by the wheel changes direction at its top and its bottom, the rider will feel lighter at the top of the ride and heavier at the bottom.

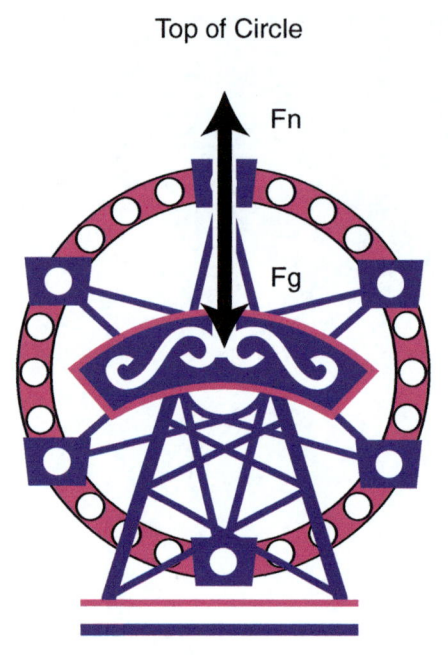

Top of Circle

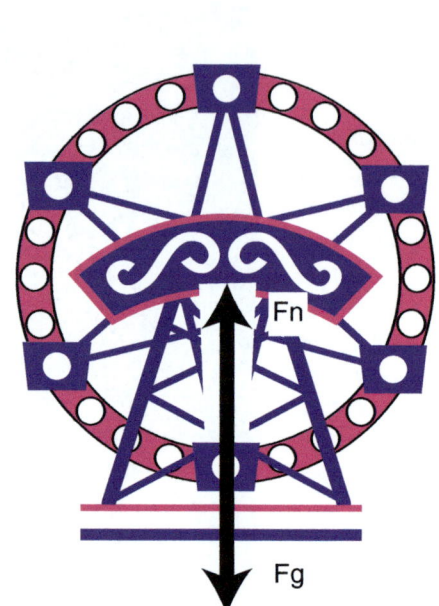

Bottom of Circle

that the capsules are actually on top of the wheel at the highest point in their journey, giving passengers a spectacular unobstructed view in all directions. Gravity helps keep the bottom of the capsules pointing downward, but an advanced stability control system was installed to make sure that the cars remain horizontal at all times.

Maintaining the balance of the cars provided a challenge for designers. If all twenty-five people inside a car were to gather on one side, a system had to be developed to keep the car in check. Computer systems detect when the cars may be out of balance and make corrections in the mounting device that supports each capsule.

Construction

The Millennium Wheel's location meant that it had to be built right on the river. The wheel is very large and located in a dense urban area, so it was not feasible to build it (and leave it partially assembled) in an upright position during construction. The rim components were sent down the river on a barge and were assembled on pontoons floating on the river. When assembly was near completion, the entire structure was slowly lifted into position by crane at a rate of only two degrees per hour. When the structure reached an angle of sixty-five degrees, it was kept there for a week until engineers had prepared it for a second lift that brought the entire wheel to a vertical position.

Architectural marvels of recent years are a testament to the courage and creativity of their designers. They are also proof of the range of design innovation around the world, all of which (to greater or lesser extents) builds on the knowledge gained in previous centuries. The Millennium Wheel and the Gateway Arch, for example, are not new building types

A detailed view of a compartment of the Millennium Wheel seen at dusk.

MODERN WONDERS

ROLLER COASTERS

Another popular amusement park ride, the roller coaster, operates entirely differently from a Ferris wheel. A roller coaster consists of several linked passenger cars that run on a looping track, typically at very high speeds. The coaster cars do not have individual engines. The only part of the ride that requires powered assistance is at the very beginning when the cars are usually tugged up a steep incline. By the time they reach the top, they have a supply of potential energy. This energy is then given off as kinetic energy when the cars make their first exhilarating rush down the incline or into a loop. The ride usually alternates between ups and downs to keep up this exchange of energy. Each time the cars slow as they go up a hill, they have converted their kinetic energy into potential energy, which is then converted back into kinetic energy as they speed down the other side. Toward the end of the ride, there is less potential energy available to the cars because the inclines and drops become smaller and smaller. Along the entire ride, some energy is also lost to the friction force between the cars and the tracks. Once the cars completely run out of potential energy, the ride ends.

but are examples of existing forms taken to a new level. Technology made the Eiffel Tower possible, while ice hotels use primarily natural materials assembled in a completely new way. These modern wonders frame our cities and create the beautiful skylines that have become emblematic of society's devotion to innovative engineering.

GLOSSARY

Angular velocity—the speed at which an object rotates, combined with the direction in which it is rotating

Axial force—a force acting along an axis (i.e., perpendicular to the cross-section of an object), such as the force of gravity on a vertical object

Axle—the central support of a wheel; spokes that provide tension in the wheel connect to the axle

Carbon steel—an iron-steel alloy that comes in different combinations of the two materials

Catenary curve—the name for the shape of the curve that is formed when a heavy chain, or necklace, is held by two points and allowed to droop in the center

Chord—the horizontal component of a truss

Circumference—the distance around the perimeter of a circle

Cladding—the exterior shell of a building that protects inhabitants from weather

Compression—the squeezing together of two structural elements due to an external force

Construction documents—drawings detailing every aspect of a building and how it should be built

Creeper cranes—specially designed cranes that crawled up the vertical elevator tracks of the Eiffel Tower and the St. Louis Arch to aid in construction

GLOSSARY

Crystalline solid—a type of solid composed of crystals that are formed in a repeating pattern

Curvilinear design—a type of design in which curved lines, rather than straight ones, provide the basis for the project

Damper—any material or object the purpose of which is to dampen (reduce) vibrations

Deconstructionism—initially a way of interpreting philosophy and literature by breaking down individual paragraphs, lines, and phrases into their composite elements; this method was later applied to architecture

Dry ice—frozen carbon dioxide

Electromagnetic spectrum—a way of referring to a range of different types of electromagnetic radiation, which spans a range from short-wavelength, high-energy ultraviolet, and X-rays, to visible light in the middle, longer-wavelength microwaves, and eventually radio waves

Equilateral triangle—a triangle with three equal sides

Equilibrium—a state whereby opposing forces are in balance with each other

Erosion—the action of wind and water that wears away a surface

Facade—exterior skin of a building

Friction—the force of resistance that is caused by two objects rubbing against each other

Frieze—horizontal band of sculpture that was present on the exterior of many Greek and Roman temples, arches, and other monumental architecture

Function—in mathematics, an equation that relates inputs to outputs

Gas—any matter with no established volume, shape, or size

Granite—an igneous rock consisting of quartz, feldspar, and mica

Gravitational force—the attraction between bodies as a result of their mass

Gravitational potential energy—the potential energy resulting from an object's vertical height above the surface of the earth

Hyperbola—a curve that is created by the intersection of a cone and a plane that is placed perpendicular to the base of the cone

Igloo—a dome-shaped house or other building made of compacted snow

Igneous rock—rock created from heat, usually from a melted material

Keystone—the central wedge-shaped stone in a stone arch

Kinetic energy—the energy of a body in motion

Landfill—a dump or waste disposal site; can also refer to a wet or low-lying site that has been filled in with rubble or dirt excavated elsewhere, to create new

GLOSSARY

buildable land. Such areas can be unstable in earthquakes and prone to subsidence.

Lattice—a configuration of elements that intersect or overlap in order to form a pattern

Limestone—a type of sedimentary rock widely used in the construction industry

Liquid—any matter that flows and adapts its shape to that of the container that holds it

Mica—the name for a collection of minerals that when cut will easily split into thin sheets

Mica schist—a variant of mica that also consists of quartz and feldspar

Modulus of elasticity—stress (the force causing a deformation, or bending) divided by strain (how much the object has deviated from its original shape)

Momentum—the mass of an object times its velocity

Phase change—the transition of matter from one state to another, such as from solid to liquid

Pig iron—raw iron that has been cast into a roughly shaped bar, called a pig

Pontoon—a floating, buoyant object (such as a boat), the purpose of which is to support a weight

Post-and-beam construction—a method of construction where posts (vertical members) and beams (horizontal members) are aligned so that they support the weight of a building's cladding and roof structure

Potential energy—the stored energy held by a body

Prestressed steel—steel that has artificial loads applied to it so that when placed into position and under the actual material loads, the steel bends slightly and compresses into the desired position

Puddled iron—a high-quality form of iron created from pig iron

Radio wave—a long-wavelength component of the electromagnetic spectrum

Rectilinear—consisting primarily of straight lines

Redundant structure—a building that has more structural support than what is required to simply support the building; *also*, systems built to serve as backup in the event of a partial structural failure

Resonant material—material that vibrates easily when exposed to sound waves

Rivet—a metal pin with a large head at one end, designed to connect two or more objects together

Section modulus—a value that comes from the dimensions of the steel section; used in calculating the size and number of steel members required for a structural component

GLOSSARY

Settlement—the way a building sinks into the foundation soil over time

Solid—any matter with a definitive volume, shape, and size

Specular reflection—the term for what occurs when a beam of light encounters a reflective surface, then bounces off that surface at a constant angle

Stainless steel—high-grade steel with a low carbon content

Strain—the degree to which an object has deviated from its original shape

Stress—the force that causes deformation or bending

Tension—the pulling apart of two structural elements caused by an external force

Tension spokes—very thin metal rods that lead from the central axle area to the outer rim of a wheel like a Ferris wheel

Tie rod—a bar that carries a tension force that helps keep the rim of a wheel, such as a Ferris wheel, in a stable position

Truss—a stable configuration of metal rods, or a framework of beams that is shaped to form a rigid structure

Vacuum—a volume that contains a complete absence of matter and therefore has no pressure

Vault—a three-dimensional arched structure that generally forms either the roof or sometimes the entire structure of a building

Vierendeel truss—a type of truss with stiff lower and upper beams with a vertical column connecting them; different from a traditional truss in that it has no diagonal members

Viscoelastic—a shock-absorbing material

Work—any force exerted over a distance, which causes an object to change positions

FIND OUT MORE

Books

Anderson, Normal. *Ferris Wheels: An Illustrated History.* Madison, WI: Popular Press, 1993.

Bardhan-Quallen, Sudipta. *Great Structures in History: The Eiffel Tower.* Chicago: Kidhaven, 2005.

Doherty, Craig, and Katherine Doherty. *Building America: Gateway Arch.* Chicago: Blackbirch Press, 1995.

El Croquis. *Frank Gehry, 1987–2003.* Madrid: El Croquis, 2006.

Escobar, Carole, ed. *Amusement Park Physics.* College Park, MD: American Association of Physics Teachers, 1994.

Fromonot, Francoise. *Jorn Utzon: The Sydney Opera House.* London: Phaidon Press, 2002.

Makkonen, L. *Ice and Construction.* London: Taylor and Francis, 1994.

Petroski, Henry. *Remaking the World: Adventures in Engineering.* New York: Vintage, 1998.

Sorkin, Michael. *After the World Trade Center: Rethinking New York City.* London: Routledge, 2002.

Strickland, Carol. *The Annotated Arch: A Crash Course in the History of Architecture.* Riverside, NJ: Andrews McMeel, 2001.

FIND OUT MORE

Web sites

Ask Dr. Math: http://mathforum.org/dr.math

Gehry Technologies: www.gehrytechnologies.com

London Eye: www.londoneye.com

Mount Rushmore, American Experience: www.pbs.org/wgbh/amex/rushmore

Otis Elevator: www.otis.com

Ove Arup and Partners: www.arup.com/index.cfm

Paris.org: www.paris.org

Peter Eisenman: www.eisenmanarchitects.com

Saint-Gobain: www.saint-gobain.com

The Shape of the Eiffel Tower: www.idi.ntnu.no/emner/tdt4215/collections/eiffel/11/11.htm

Snow Crystals: www.its.caltech.edu/~atomic/snowcrystals

World Trade Center: www.wtc.com

World Trade Center Site Memorial Competition: www.wtcsitememorial.org

Zaha Hadid: www.zaha-hadid.com

INDEX

Page numbers in italics refer to illustrations.

Acoustics
  Sydney Opera House, *39*, 42
  Walt Disney Concert Hall, 44, 46, 47
Aesthetics
  Arc de Triomphe, 34
  Eiffel Tower, 7–8, *8*, 10, *11*, 15, *15*
  Guggenheim Museum, 43
  ice hotels, 51, 56, 58
  Ice Palace, 60
  Louvre pyramid, 20, *20*, 21, *21*
  Roman aqueducts, *22*, 23
  St. Louis Gateway Arch, *26*, 28–29, *29*
  Sydney Opera House, *39*, 42
  translucent concrete, 48–49
  TWA Terminal, *24*, 25
  Walt Disney Concert Hall, 44, 45, *46*, *46*, 47
  World Trade Center, *62*, 75
Alcohol, freezing point of, 59
Alta Igloo Hotel, 57
Anchor bolts, 10–11, *11*
Aqueducts, *22*, 23
Arc de Triomphe, 33–34, *33*, 35

Arches
  Arc de Triomphe, 33–34, *33*, 35
  Arche de la Défense, *34*, 35
  keystones, 28, 54
  Roman Empire, *22*, 23, 34
  TWA Terminal, *24*, 25
  See also St. Louis Gateway Arch
Axial forces, 11, *11*
Axles, 93, 97, 99

Bedrock, 25, 70, 81–82
Bendable concrete, 48
Bending, 29–30
  See also Stress forces
Borglum, Gutzon, 80, 81, *81*, 83, *84*
Bridges, 16–17, *16*, 48, 67

Carbon steel, 29
Catenary curves, 30–32, *31*
Centripetal motion, 96–97, *100*
Chords, *68*, 69
Circumference, 95
Cladding and facades
  Arche de la Défense, 35
  Eiffel Tower, absent for, 8–9

Guggenheim Museum, 44
Louvre pyramid, 20–21, *20*, *21*
post-and-beam construction, 37
St. Louis Gateway Arch, 28, 29, *29*
Statue of Liberty, 17, 18
Sydney Opera House, *36*, *40*, 42
titanium, 44, 48
Walt Disney Concert Hall, 44, 45, *46*
World Trade Center, 66, *66*, *67*, 68
Compression. *See* Stress forces
Computer modeling software, 37, 39, 43, *43*
Concrete construction
  Arche de la Défense, 35
  corrosion, 85
  Eiffel Tower, 10
  new materials, 48–49
  Pentagon, 77
  St. Louis Gateway Arch, 25
  Sydney Opera House, 42
  World Exposition Ferris Wheel, 93
  World Trade Center, 66–67, *66*, *67*, 68, 70

INDEX

Construction documents, 38–39
Cranes, 11–12, 26, 28
Creeper cranes, 12, 26, 28
Crude iron, 9
Crystal Palace, 18–19
Crystalline structures, *52, 53, 55,* 81
Curvilinear design
  deconstructionism, 41, *41*
  Guggenheim Museum, 43, *43*
  new materials, 47–49
  "straight" structures, contrasted with, 37–39, *38,* 44
  Sydney Opera House, *36,* 39–40, *39, 40,* 42
  Walt Disney Concert Hall, 44–46, *46,* 47
  See also Arches; Ferris wheels

Dampers, 68, *68,* 69
Deconstructionism, 41, *41*
Double-wall construction, 26
Dry ice, 53

Eiffel, Alexandre-Gustave, *6,* 16–17
Eiffel Tower
  construction, *6,* 7–8, 11–13, 14
  design, 7–11, *8, 9, 10, 11*
  elevators, 13–14, *13,* 15
  famous copies, 18–19, *19*
  function, 8, 14–15
  maintenance, 15, *15*
Eiffel Tower of London, 18–19
Eisenman, Peter, 41
Electromagnetic spectrum, 14
Elevators and trams
  Eiffel Tower, 13–14, *13,* 15
  Mount Rushmore, 83
  St. Louis Gateway Arch, 26, 28, 32–33
Energy, potential, 73, 74, 94, 95, 102
Equations. *See* Mathematical equations
Equilateral triangles, 28
Equilibrium, 54

Erosion, 81–82, 85
Excavations, 10, 64–66, 70

Facades. *See* Cladding and facades
Ferris wheels
  early construction, 92–95, *92*
  layout and physics, 91, 95–97, *96, 100*
  Millennium Wheel, *90,* 98–101, *99, 101*
  portable wheels, 97
  triple wheels, 98
Fire safety, 69
Foundations
  Arche de la Défense, 35
  Eiffel Tower, 10–11, *11*
  Pentagon, 77
  portable Ferris wheels, 97
  St. Louis Gateway Arch, 25, 28, 32
  Sydney Opera House, 42
  World Exposition Ferris Wheel, 93
  World Trade Center, 66, *66,* 70
Freedom Tower, 74
Friction, 69, 96, 102
Friezes, 34

Gas phase, 52, 53
  See also Steam engines
Gateway Arch. *See* St. Louis Gateway Arch
Gehry, Frank, 42–47, *43, 46*
Geology, 81–82
Glass facades
  Guggenheim Museum, 44
  Louvre pyramid, 20–21, *20, 21*
  Sydney Opera House, *40*
  Walt Disney Concert Hall, 44
  World Trade Center, 68
Granite, 35, 42, 81–82
Gravitational forces
  Ferris wheels, 94, 95–97, 100, *100*
  how the Twin Towers fell, 73–74

St. Louis Gateway Arch, 30, 31
Guggenheim Museum, 43, *43*

Hadid, Zaha, 41
Hall of Records, 85
Hyperbolas, 31

Ice, properties of, 52–53, *52,* 54
Ice hotels
  aesthetics, 51, 56, 58
  Alta Igloo Hotel, 57
  Ice Hotel Quebec, 58, *58*
  Jukkasjärvi Ice Hotel, *50,* 55–57, *55, 56, 57*
Ice Palace, 60–61, *61*
Igloos, 53–55, *54,* 56
  See also Ice hotels
Igneous rock, 81, 82
Iron construction
  carbon steel, 29
  Eiffel Tower, 9, 10, *10,* 11, 12–13
  Ponte Maria Bridge, *16,* 17
  Statue of Liberty, 17, 18

Jefferson, Thomas, 80, 88, *89*
Jukkasjärvi Ice Hotel, *50,* 55–57, *55, 56, 57*

Keystones, 28, 54
Kiev television tower, 18
Kinetic energy, 74, 95, 102

Landfill, 65, 70
Lattices
  Eiffel Tower, 9–10
  ice crystals, *52, 53,* 55
  Statue of Liberty, 18
  See also Trusses
Light reflection, 45, *45*
Lighting
  Eiffel Tower, 15, *15*
  igloos, 54
  translucent concrete, 48–49
  Walt Disney Concert Hall, 44
Limestone, 10, 44, 77
Lincoln, Abraham, *78,* 80, *84,* 88, *89*

INDEX

Liquids, 52, 53, 59
Loads. *See* Stress forces
London Eye. *See* Millennium Wheel
Louvre pyramid, 20–21, *20, 21*

Mathematical equations
  Ferris wheels, 95, 96–97
  freezing point of alcohol, 59
  Gateway Arch, 30–32
  how the Twin Towers fell, 73–74
  light reflection, 45
  modulus of elasticity, 48
Mica, 81, 82
Millennium Wheel, *90,* 98–101, *99, 101*
Modernism, *39,* 40
Modulus of elasticity, 48
Momentum, 74
Mount Rushmore National Memorial
  construction, 82–88, *83, 84, 86*
  design, 79, 80–81, *81,* 87–89
  maintenance, *78*

Nice Observatory, 17

Ohio State University Wexner Center, 41

Panama Canal, 17
Parabola curves, 30–31, *31,* 32
Parisian La Ruche, 17
Pei, I.M., 20–21, *20, 21*
Pentagon, 76–77, *76, 77*
Phase changes, 12, 52, 53
Pig iron, 9
Ponte Maria Bridge, 16–17, *16*
Pontoons, 100
Portable Ferris wheels, 97
Positional potential energy, 73–74, 94
Post-and-beam construction, 37–38, *38,* 44
Potential energy, 73, 74, 94, 95, 102

Prestressed steel, 25
Puddled iron, 9, 10

Radio transmitters, 14–15, 19
Redundant structures, 71
Resonant materials, 47
Rivets, 12–13
Roller coasters, 102
Roman construction, *22,* 23, 34, 38
Roosevelt, Theodore, 80, 89, *89*
Rosenthal Center for Contemporary Art, 41, *41*

Saarinen, Eero, 24–25, *24*
  See also St. Louis Gateway Arch
Safety
  Eiffel Tower, 12, 14
  Ferris wheels, 97, 98, 100
  Mount Rushmore, 87
  Pentagon, *76,* 77
  World Trade Center, 66, 69, 71
St. Louis Gateway Arch
  construction, 25–26, *27,* 28
  design, 23–26, *26,* 28–33, *29,* 35
  tram, 26, 32–33
Section modulus, 30
Settlement, 70
Shear resistance. *See* Wind resistance
Shifted grids, 41
Sky Whirl, 98
Snow houses, 53–55, *54,* 56
  See also Ice hotels
Solids, 52, 53
Sound. *See* Acoustics
Specular reflection, 45, *45*
Spreckelsen, Johann Otto von, 35
Stainless steel facades
  St. Louis Gateway Arch, 28, 29, *29*
  Walt Disney Concert Hall, 44, 45, *46*
Statue of Liberty, 17, *17,* 18
Steam engines, 11–12, 13, 94–95
Steel construction
  Arche de la Défense, 35

  corrosion, 85
  Ferris wheels, 93–94, 97
  Guggenheim Museum, 44
  iron, compared to, 10
  Kiev tower, 18
  Louvre pyramid, 21, *21*
  St. Louis Gateway Arch, 25–26, 28, 29–30, *29*
  Sydney Opera House, 42
  Walt Disney Concert Hall, 44, 45, *46*
  World Trade Center, 66–68, *66, 68,* 69, 71, 73–74
Stress forces
  bendable concrete, 48
  Eiffel Tower, 10, *10,* 11, *11*
  Ferris wheels, 94, 95–97, 100, *100*
  geological conditions, 81–82
  Guggenheim Museum, 44
  igloos, 54
  post-and-beam construction, 37–38, *38,* 44
  St. Louis Gateway Arch, 25, 29–32
  Statue of Liberty, 18
  titanium, 48
  World Trade Center, *66,* 68–69, *68,* 71–74, *72*
Sydney Opera House, *36,* 39–40, *39, 40,* 42

Tension spokes, 97
Tension. *See* Stress forces
Tie rods, 99
Titanium, 44, 48, 85
Trams. *See* Elevators and trams
Translucent concrete, 48–49
Triangle forms, 20–21, *20, 21,* 28–29
Triple Ferris wheels, 98
Trusses
  Eiffel Tower, 9, 11, *11*
  St. Louis Gateway Arch, 28
  World Trade Center, 66–69, *66, 67, 68*
  See also Lattices

INDEX

TWA Terminal, *24*, 25
Twin Towers. *See* World Trade Center

Utzon, Jorn, 39–40, 42

Vaccums, 12
Vaults, 42, 58
Vierendeel trusses, 67–69, *67*
Viscoelastic materials, *68*, 69
Vitra Fire Station, 41
Vodka, freezing point of, 59

Walt Disney Concert Hall, 44–46, *46*, 47
Washington, George, 80, 88, *89*
Wavelengths, 14–15, 47
Wexner Center, 41
Wind resistance
 Eiffel Tower, 10, *10*
 World Trade Center, *66*, 68–69, *68*, 71
Wooden interiors, 42, 44, 46, *46*, 47
Work, 94, 95

World Trade Center
 aesthetic design, *62*, 75
 construction, 64–68, *65*, *66*, *67*, 70
 structural design, 63–64, *64*, 66–70, *66*, *67*
 terrorist attacks, 70, 71–75, *72*

9780765682000